Men of the Mutiny

Men of the Mutiny

Two Accounts of the
Great Indian Mutiny of 1857

Fighting with the Bengal Yeomanry Cavalry
John Tulloch Nash

Private Metcalfe at Lucknow
Henry Metcalfe

LEONAUR

Men of the Mutiny: Two Accounts of the
Great Indian Mutiny of 1857
Fighting with the Bengal Yeomanry Cavalry by John Tulloch Nash
Private Metcalfe at Lucknow by Henry Metcalfe

First published under the titles
Volunteering in India 1893
and
Chronicle of Private Metcalfe

Leonaur is an imprint of Oakpast Ltd

Copyright in this form © 2009 Oakpast Ltd

ISBN: 978-1-84677-624-3 (hardcover)
ISBN: 978-1-84677-623-6 (softcover)

http://www.leonaur.com

Contents

Fighting with the Bengal YeomanryCavalry

John Tulloch Nash

Contents

THE BENGAL YEOMANRY CAVALRY VOLUNTEERS
IN THE INDIAN MUTINY CAMPAIGN, 1857-1858

In Memoriam

Dedicated to the Beloved Memory of General Joseph Nash, C.B., a Man Esteemed by All With Whom He Came in Contact, and Who Passed a Life-Long Military Career in Serving His Country With Rare Distinction and Honour,
By
His Eldest Son, the Author, Late of the Bengal Yeomanry Cavalry.

Preface

In the following narrative an attempt has been made to relate the military services of the Bengal Yeomanry Cavalry during the Indian Mutiny, and Sepoy War; and as truth lies in a small compass, so this little volume contains no fiction, nor will any conjectural narration be found in its compressed chapters of unembellished facts.

Parenthetically, it may be recorded in this place that, as the Bengal Yeomanry Cavalry was the parent, or pioneer corps, of the great Patriotic Force now established and consolidated in England, it is entitled to claim the proud distinction of having undeniably originated the modern Volunteer movement throughout the British Empire, and this narrative will tend to show that the corps was worthy of that proud position.

Although more than thirty years have elapsed since the "transitory regiment" passed away with the shifting tide of events, the subjoined narrative is the legitimate offspring of my manuscript journal, kept with diligence and care at the time when the various movements, scenes, and actions it describes occurred.

Nevertheless, the mere fact of my having kept this journal as a sealed book up to the present day, conclusively proves that I never intended to publish its contents, nor did I anticipate ever being asked by the gallant survivors (there are, alas! few now left) of my late fellow-volunteers to allow it to be published. They, however, see that a Volunteer Age has dawned upon the world since the eventful year 1857; and lest in the gigantic strides of the general movement the eminent services they rendered to their country in the darkest days of the Mutiny fade into oblivion, and be lost to them altogether, they naturally seek a descriptive record—an authoritative biography, as it were—to perpetuate the military operations in which they were engaged. I have accordingly traced an unassuming sketch of those familiar operations; and my readers must never lose sight of the fact that the Government Gazetted records—which are quoted in this plain, unvarnished narrative—substantiate, in every detail, the veracity of every paragraph I have written. And as regards all that concerns the rough composition of my pages, I have to ask some forbearance, for they but reflect, as in a glass, the contents of a journal penned not merely in the days of my youth, but also amid the interminable stir of a Mutiny never likely to be forgotten by those who bore the first shock of it, and passed through its fearful horrors.

London, 1893.

CHAPTER 1

The Red Year

1857 are figures indelibly dyed in blood, and their sanguinary impression stamps one of the most cruel, and sorrowful pages in the history of the world.

In that disastrous year of the Indian Mutiny—which even to the present day continues to furnish authentic material for the revelation of almost unknown episodes appertaining to that memorable period—the following abstract of Notification No. 931, dated July 23rd, 1857, was published by the Government of India:—

The Governor-General in Council has reason to know that there are in Calcutta, Bengal, and the North-West Provinces many Englishmen whose peaceable avocations have been interrupted by the disturbed state of the country, and who, although in no way connected with the Government, are willing and eager to give an active support to its authority at the present time by sharing service in the Field with the troops of the Queen, and of the East India Company.

The Governor-General in Council has thorough confidence in the loyalty, courage, and enterprising zeal of the community to which he refers, and he is satisfied that service rendered in the spirit in which they are ready to give it will be most valuable to the State.

With the view of availing himself of such service in the most effectual manner, his Lordship in Council directs that a Volunteer Corps of cavalry be formed, to be called the Bengal Yeomanry Cavalry, and to be equipped and prepared for duty in the disturbed districts, etc., etc.

At this critical time of national gloom, when there was mourning throughout the length and breadth of England, and Upper India was saturated with the innocent blood of our hapless fellow-countrymen, Volunteers—amid great demonstrations of enthusiasm—cheerfully responded to the appeal contained in the above-quoted notification, and within a week of its publication a cavalry regiment—composed not of "European adventurers and Eurasians," as was at first surmised, but of young military officers recently arrived from England, or those left idle by the mutiny of their regiments, of clerks in the Government and mercantile offices, of midshipmen belonging to the Peninsular and Oriental and other companies' ships, of indigo planters, of some unemployed Europeans and Eurasians, of young men related to the best families in the country; and most of these were excellent riders, good shots, and keen sportsmen—was actually formed, mounted, equipped, and ready for service in the field.

Accordingly, on an appointed day, at an early hour the Corps rode forth, and drew up on the Calcutta esplanade for inspection by the Governor-General.

But as the morning had not yet sufficiently brightened for the "review," I took advantage of the idle moments at my disposal to note on the margin of my shirt-cuff the uniform, or rather "turn-out," of the Volunteers.

They wore brown corduroy breeches, over which were drawn jack-boots reaching above the knees; loose blue flannel blouses (called "jumpers" by the diggers in Australia); and grey felt helmets enveloped in huge white turbans completed a rough-and-ready uniform, in which they certainly looked a dashing and dare-devil set of fellows. A heavy sabre, light carbine, and formidable revolvers were their arms.

The horses, though untrained, were young, powerful, and splendid animals for the hard and unceasing work they were destined to encounter. And their trappings were for service, and not for show.

The Governor-General (Lord Canning), having inspected and complimented the Volunteers, bade them a kind farewell a sincere *au revoir*. And presently the Corps, numbering two hundred and fifty-eight sabres, under the leadership of Colonel Richardson, C.B., left Calcutta for Upper India.

Two hundred and fifty-eight volunteers seem a paltry number to have rallied round the Government in so momentous a crisis as that which called them to arms on its behalf; but it must be borne in mind that in those awful days there were but a mere handful of available Englishmen in Bengal, and so far as their numbers were concerned, it was an acknowledged surprise that so many were found to leap forward in aid of the state. Besides, during the Mutiny, it was not so much the force of numbers as the dreaded calm white face, with the avenging sword in hand, that made its presence terrible whenever and wherever it appeared before the mutineers. Moreover, the reader must not forget that it was impossible to overvalue the worth of an Englishman in those critical times. His very shadow was a tower of strength. And animated by a thorough sense of patriotism, and relying upon our own personal efforts, with unbounded confidence in each other, we were worth our number ten times told.

Chapter 2

The March

From Calcutta the corps, having been ferried across the river Hughly to Howrah, was conveyed by railway in a few hours to Raneegung, over the first stage on its onward journey.

Raneegung—then the terminus of the East Indian Railway—was at that period a great rendezvous of the army proceeding to the seat of the war, and warlike preparations on a formidable scale were going on there with amazing rapidity. Masses of troops, horses for cavalry and artillery, baggage animals, immense parks of guns, magazine and commissariat stores, countless *dolies* or hospital litters, camp equipage and innumerable busy followers, demonstrated the unrelenting realities and stern agitation of the times.

But all this bustle and chaos did not trouble us long; for before we could realise by the warlike scenes around us our sudden transformation from civilians to soldiers, we were "told off" to join a force proceeding to the North-West Provinces.

At midnight therefore we stood to arms in readiness to march. In front of all were to move several companies of European infantry, having a troop of horse-artillery in immediate communication with them: they were to be followed by us and the "us," I may remark, means, and always will mean in this narrative, the Bengal Yeomanry Cavalry the whole being covered by a native regiment of the Madras army as a rear guard. The line of march having thus been formed, the bugles rang out the "advance," and away we moved.

Our route lay along that famous Grand Trunk Road leading to the North-West Provinces, and on its smooth metallic surface men and animals, fresh from the first cantonment, swung along at a smart pace, and reached the halting ground as the crowing of farmyard tenantry proclaimed the commencement of dawn. Here to our yet inexperienced eyes the change was striking. Tents were pitched, arms piled, sentries posted, fires kindled, breakfasts served in short, the whole force, with its long train of camp followers and beasts of burden, settled down at ease; whilst amid the novelty and routine of camp life the day glided away pleasantly enough, and at eventide retiring to rest in good time, men slept soundly and refreshed themselves for the morrow's work. So, in a word, began and closed the first march at the opening of our campaign.

At the break of day on the following morning the march of the force began again, and was conducted in the same manner as before, until a portion of it was suddenly detached from the main body in order to pursue mutineers through Sonthalistan. Of course hurried inquiries into the cause of this change in our pre-arranged route at once passed along the line; but as suspicious tidings of disaffection among the sepoys at Deoghur had reached Raneegung before our departure from thence, we did not receive any very unlooked-for communication when it was told us that the garrison had mutinied at that outlandish cantonment.

A lightly equipped column—formed of European infantry and ourselves—soon therefore entered that wild and uninteresting country of the aboriginal Sonthals, who, although their homes lay in so isolated and apparently tiger-haunted a region, seemed happy and contented with their lot. From stage to stage they cheerfully supplied the commissariat with ample provisions, and this was all the more surprising as for days together we traversed almost barren hills and dense jungles. Nevertheless the lowlands were exceedingly fertile, while horned cattle and sheep and domestic poultry appeared abundant in many of the villages through which we passed.

The column having at length threaded its way through a considerable portion of this savage-looking country, gained a breakneck road leading to a plateau on which the station of Deoghur stood. And here, for the first time, we beheld and bore witness to the influence of the appalling whirlwind of desolation that was passing over India.

Deoghur itself lay enwrapped in sepulchral silence of death, and all that was once the military cantonments in ruins and ashes; while in a well-kept garden close by, the faithful! domestic servants (who had buried their murdered masters) pointed out to us the recent graves of those who had fallen a sacrifice to the relentless fury of the bloodthirsty Sepoys. They also told us that on that fatal spot a few loyal Sepoys actually killed some of the mutineers in defence of their officers.

Although many days had elapsed since the departure of the mutineers from Deoghur, still the hope of intercepting the fiends stimulated pursuit, and onwards we pressed. Over the hilly tracks, along execrable roads, through leafy labyrinths, down deep arid broad ravines, for several wearisome days we traversed long and rapid marches, but all to no purpose. The pursuit proved ineffectual, the expedition fruitless. The start of the fugitives was too great; and unencumbered with baggage or other impedimenta, they easily escaped towards the North-West Provinces.

While struggling to overtake these mutineers, we were attacked by that mortal scourge, curse, and blight of India and the most terrible enemy in the world the cholera, and as its assault often begins with death, a few members of the corps fell victims to its attack.

By this time having fairly spanned Sonthalistan, and pioneered our way along the plains beyond it, we debouched from straggling villages into a lonely road, where a milestone pillar set up at the junction of several zigzag paths indexed the distance to "Holy Gyah," according to the inscription, four miles; so we inarched on, and finally fording a broad and shallow stream, entered that "venerated town," to find that even so "sacred" a place of pilgrimage had not escaped the mischievous villainy of scoundrels, revelling in the wanton destruction of property, and in all kinds of devilry.

Throughout the Bengal Presidency, Gyah is known and reverenced by the Hindus as a holy town, replete with hallowed mythological traditions; and, in a sentence, a "holy town" in India means a place crammed with quaint temples and grotesque shrines, where astounding idolatry reigns supreme, where pilgrims flock in crowds all the year round, and where those insolent and painted vagabonds, the pagan priests, luxuriate and fatten on the superstitious liberality of a bigoted and deluded people, while under pretences of sanctimonious priestcraft, they cloak sensual intrigue and sin with impunity. At the same time, however, they maintain as numberless priests of other nationalities maintain that they are not necessarily bound, because they are priests, to live and lead the lives of saints!

Whatever charms of antiquity Gyah may have possessed, we had no time to explore them; for immediately on our arrival there, we prepared to start in pursuit of another body of mutineers hovering about the districts bordering on the frontier of Nipal.

CHAPTER 3

The Advance

The necessary arrangements for long marches having been rapidly completed, we turned our backs on the "holy town," and started for Patna along a pleasant road that lay by the side of vast plains concealed with sprouting corn, and in places fringed with immense belts of trees and evergreen shrubs, which only disappeared when we entered an avenue of miles in extent leading into Patna.

To speak of silvan avenues as stretching miles in extent, would seem to imply that they had been measured with the proverbial "long bow"; but in passing, it may be mentioned that in many parts of India magnificent avenues stretch scores of miles without a break.

The town of Patna, though large, is in no wise very remarkable. It contains, however, an immense population of disloyal Mahommedans, and is one of the great centres of disaffection and intrigue in India. Situated on the right bank of the Ganges, it presents a rather prepossessing panoramic view of an Oriental riverside town; and viewed from the water it is a long, irregular line of countless buildings closely packed together in grotesque shapes of various sizes, while prominently visible in its midst are some picturesque mosques, and a huge bell-shaped building, with a winding outer staircase leading to the top.

We crossed the Ganges at Patna. The river was at its lowest level; still the passage, beginning with dawn glimmering upon our difficulties, continued the whole of the day, and did not terminate before the shadows of eventide compelled us to bivouac on its bank opposite the town. And here we endeavoured to make ourselves as comfortable for the night as circumstances would allow, in a wretched encampment teeming with mosquitoes and frogs, and reeking with malaria exhaled from putrid vegetation on the margin of the river.

But now no more sombre thoughts, for sleep cradled in the arms of fatigue had lulled dull care to rest; while all life, too, reposed in the quietude of a serenely lovely night, and nothing but the monotonous clink of the sentinels' scabbards, trailing along the ground as they paced to and fro, stirred the profound silence of the slumbering camp.

On the following morning as the sun rose, we rose too, and the forward movement began through a country in general feature similar to that we had recently traversed, but apparently without any signs of anarchy in it. In fact, there was nothing to indicate a hostile country; and in proof of its tranquillity, over the vast expanse of the plains, as far as the scope of vision, on every side corn was sprouting in the greatest exuberance; and commissariat supplies were found in abundance at every stage. Without therefore encountering any obstacle on our line of march, we reached the little town of Pusah worthy of notice only on account of the enormous stud of horses it contained.

Meanwhile the alarming rumours relating to the mutineers—of whom mention has already been made— rendered it necessary for us to halt at Pusah, until reliable intelligence could be received in place of the numerous and exaggerated reports that were in circulation within and around the neighbouring districts. Some rumours asserted that the revolted troops were on their way to loot the Government stud; others declared that they had broken away through the adjoining country; while a few maintained, and with truth, as the sequel will show, that they were in a "fix" for want of boats on the impetuous river that barred their way to the Upper Provinces.

Our "forced halts" at Pusah afforded an opportunity for re-organising the transport train, which was found defective for forced marches. And instead of that "awful machine," the country cart, yoked to crawling bullocks that ordinarily averaged a "motion" of two or three miles an hour, and accomplished a distance of three or four leagues a day, and that only under the influence of perpetual and tremendous shouting, barbarous castigation, and tails twisted into corkscrews until the joints cracked, elephants and those hardy animals the pack-ponies were substituted for the conveyance of the baggage.

While we remained encamped at Pusah, among other means adopted to beguile the weary hours, races and steeplechases were "got up"; and as the place had an excellent course, and the weather was delightful and exhilarating, the pastime helped to dispel grumblings, and in some instances imaginary grievances which inaction had commenced to sew.

So passed a few days, each of which brought with it both its amusements and its anxieties. Before a week had terminated, however, it was evident by the hurry-skurry prevailing in the striking of tents and packing of baggage that an immediate headlong rush to the Nipal frontier was in store for us. So we started at once, and jogged along throughout the night, and by daylight, finding the baggage animals keeping well up, we marched on for a few hours longer, and then halted for the day amidst a fertile country verdant with waving crops of several kinds.

I shall pass rapidly over the stages travelled during the ensuing few days, as their monotony was only dispelled on our entering the district of Purneah. Here the features of the country changed alternately from rich cultivated fields, to immense grass plains; and from those again to enormous crops of ripening scarlet chillies, which gave the whole landscape a bloodshot appearance of a singular and—as times were—very appropriate effect.

We also passed incalculable acres of poppy fields, and their variegated bloom of red, white, and purple in the golden sunlight adorned a sublimely pretty floral scene of many miles stretching along our route. And as we gazed on these fascinating fields, which in their beauty looked as if brilliantly bespangled with swarming butterflies, it was strange to realise the curious fact that in so beautiful a bloom lurked also a deadly poison. For is it not a notable fact in the opium trade that the poppy blossom not only fascinates India with its product, but demoralises, if not kills, China with its venom? while the Government piles up mountains of gold rising from the plains of "Opiumana"— to coin a name in a flowery and figurative sense—as memorial monuments typical of gratitude to both! Hence no apology is needed for my turning aside from our line of march to bestow this apparently eccentric and perhaps frivolous panegyric on those whom it may concern. But let us hope that the day may come, when the opium revenue will cease to fill the coffers of a Christian Government, at the expense and demoralisation of a heathen empire, like that of China.

When we had advanced thus far towards the confines of Nipal, the indomitable ponies began gradually to yield to the toil they had hitherto sustained stoutly, and in considerable numbers, as they staggered along under their loads, dropped by the wayside and perished; the baggage would in consequence have to be divided among that carried by yet vigorous animals, and they being thus overweighted would straggle up hours after we had bivouacked; and then the time usually occupied in serving out and cooking the rations was the most disagreeable part of the day's work; for m addition to being already well tired and desiring repose, exhausted and famished men had to superintend the preparation of unsavoury meals, and postpone rest found in sleep of which they stood sorely in need.

In this unsatisfactory way we continued to push on from one day to another, until at length the beasts of burden having been fairly beaten down, we were compelled to part with our baggage, and "stow away" upon our horses and about our own persons some indispensable things for our use on the road. And that night, after receiving many uneasy salutations in the way of *salaams* from our servants and camp followers, whose countenances showed apprehension at being forsaken, without even a guard, to follow us as best they could; we struck into a well-trodden path running over low, sterile lands in a south-easterly direction.

CHAPTER 4

The Foothills

Although at this period disaffection lurked in almost every corner of the Bengal Presidency, and the greater part of Northern India was in open rebellion, and in Oudh (except the ground at the Ahlum Bagh, in the suburbs of Luknow, on which a British force stood), not a vestige of the Government authority had yet been re-established, and albeit we were daily nearing a body of revolted troops, there were no signs of anarchy, nor any manifest feelings of hostility discernible among the people of these districts.

It is true there could be no confidence, and there was none; but the friendly disposition of the inhabitants may be considered sufficiently apparent, when the fact is stated that the rustic food and fodder supplied by them at every halt, amply provided for the pressing wants of the corps.

It were tedious, however, to relate the untoward difficulties we encountered in these flying marches, and to recount the rough-and-ready way in which we were compelled to meet the troubles of our position to hint at each volunteer personally attending to his horse; to tell of our " sleeping accommodation" for weeks together being the bare ground, screened sometimes against the heavy dews of December by leafy canopies of trees, the projecting roots of which served as extemporised pillows; to speak of the novel or unique spectacle presented in joints of mutton spitted on sabres with which the sheep had had their heads struck off grilling over huge green-wood fires, and then, half raw and well smoked, devoured without salt or sauce with a relish, not to say gusto, that Soyer himself, or even genuine cannibals, might have envied; to note that roasted rice pounded into powder with the butt-end of our carbines proved an acceptable substitute for tea or coffee; and, finally, to remark that breakfasting on parched grain, and boiled milk, was certainly not very unusual with us during these fast and furious rides.

English readers may be slightly surprised at our finding time, while rushing headlong over the country, to indulge in the oceans of boiled milk to which we were treated at these hurried *al fresco* breakfasts. But the Hindus, who supplied us never use milk not even for making butter unless it is thoroughly boiled, like water for making tea. In its raw state they consider it little better than the animal morbid matter, and often call it, by way of execration, "white blood," and believe that if it is used without undergoing purification by fire, its virus is sure to inoculate the human body with some virulent disease, or develop some malady to which it may be predisposed. Apart, however, from the open confession that, in upholding the opinion of these Hindus, I would as soon eat raw beef as drink raw milk, it may be appropriate to mention here that in all my experience of nearly thirty years in India I never knew, or heard of, a single case of diphtheria in man, woman, or child who used boiled milk; while, at the same time, I have known several Europeans, who were in the habit of taking milk as it is generally used in Europe, to die of the disease, when not a native among whom they were living, and who numbered in proportion at least a thousand to each European, showed a sign of the disease at all.

Some days having passed in the manner mentioned above, we at length gained a sandy tract, on the banks of the Kose river, where the savage scenery was impressively grand. Taking its rise among the Himalaya Mountains, the Kose, deep and impetuous, winds its course through, and emerges from, the sombre recesses of well-nigh utterly impenetrable jungle. This sub- mountain jungle is called the Terai, and it stretches along parallel to the base of the Himalaya Range, and varies in breadth, on a rough average, from ten to twenty miles.

Without noticing, however, the insignificant bit of it at present before us, I will here briefly speak of its prominent features as they appear interspersed throughout the whole of that wondrous region; so that the reader may form some idea of the nature of the country in which we were at this time employed.

Roughly though correctly sketched, either by pen or pencil, the Terai is a vast trackless belt of forest covering hundreds of miles with almost every variety of luxuriant tropical vegetation; and in innumerable) localities it is intersected by rivers, mountain-torrents, and frightful ravines choked up with thorny under-wood, and interlaced with bamboos, ratans, and other rope-like plants and creepers; and in places it is diversified with savage-looking hills densely draped in dark foliage, and timber of stupendous size; while in its midst are enormous abysses filled with putrid water and interminable swamps, which eject the poisonous streams that silently and invisibly glide like mythological serpents through this enormous jungle-entangled region.

Though the inexhaustible profusion of vegetation is the most striking and impressive feature of the Terai, its exuberance in animal life is certainly not much less characteristic; and in numbers and variety, it may be said to exhibit greater richness in the department of zoology, than any other region on the globe.

Passing over its insignificant hordes of the wild animal kingdom, I shall cursorily notice only in passing some of its more prominent denizens; and among the prolific category, enumerate the buffalo, the samber, the lilgye, and deer of several species in incalculable numbers. Then the deeper recesses of the Terai have their appropriate occupants: there the elephant, the rhinoceros, the tiger, leopards, bears, hyenas, etc., may be computed literally by thousands and thousands. The serpent species, from the formidable boa-constrictor to the dangerous cobra, abound. Among the venomous reptiles there are many varieties of huge lizards, and alligators of enormous size swarm in the streams and marshes. The feathered tribe, from the magnificent golden eagle to birds unknown in ornithology, are also numerous; while insects, infinite in variety, infest these regions in endless myriads.

The malarial climate of the Terai, however, is so deadly to Europeans that they are prevented from tarrying in its fever-breeding jungles. Were it other- wise, sportsmen in search of big game would astonish, with their "bags," the most ardent hunters in any part of the world.

Behind the Terai are the lower hills and their subsidiary dells, also covered with evergreen woods, and timber of such gigantic size that the very sight of it fills one with astonishment beyond conception,—trees of from twenty to thirty feet in girth, and, although centuries old, upright as pillars, straight as darts, and growing to a height of two hundred feet or more. Beyond, stretching like a huge irregular barrier, rise the noble Himalaya, and the lofty and fantastic peaks of the mountains enveloped in everlasting winter. To associate tropical India with the North Pole would seem ridiculously fictitious; nevertheless there, before our very eyes, tower the ice-bound giants of wonderland, which even in the height of summer freeze all the day through, despite the sun, and look down from their perpetual frozen abode upon the poor broiling creatures on the fiery plains below. While farther to the north, far above the others, to an elevation of more than twenty-eight thousand feet above sea-level, Kunchin Junga, with its majestic head right away in endless space, distinct and well defined under the clear blue canopy of heaven, looks in its incomparable grandeur like an isolated mountain of molten silver, towering to the skies from an aerial world of eternal glaciers and snow.

The spot from whence this view is obtained, and from which we were not very far bivouacked, commands the most magnificent prospect of the dazzling Snowy Range visible from any place in India. Nothing in Nature on her grandest scale can be conceived more awe-inspiring, or awfully sublime. Talk about Mont Blanc, why, that lofty snow-capped peak in Europe is, by comparison, a mere hillock to the giant Kunchin Junga in High Asia. And so prominent and stupendous is this wonderful monarch of mountains, that the indigenous mountaineers actually believe its geographical position to be as expressed in their own words the centre of the terrestrial world, and its summit, towering up to heaven, they say is half-way to the celestial realm above, whereon rests the hallowed foot- stool of the Great God of Heaven! Just as under the influence of similar superstitious nonsense, the inhabitants of the Peshawur valley, about a thousand miles or perhaps more away in the Punjab, call a snow-capped peak Tukht-i-Suleiman, or "Solomon's throne"! The Viceroy of India has also a throne on these incomparable mountains; and in consequence Simla has been the regular summer residence of Government for far more than half a century. It is, therefore, astonishing to note how little this delightful salubrious region has been opened up, and how little we really know of this vast mountainous world within itself. Now, as the atmospheric temperature on the plains of Upper India for about half the year may be compared with that of a veritable glowing furnace, it is quite distressing to find that the charms of the Himalaya—with their invigorating climate, suggestive only of the most lovely "cool summer" in England—should remain so neglected, and little better than a trackless wilderness in Africa. And that, too, when even the present wretchedly laid out and badly built old hill stations (to wit, Simla, Mussoorie, Nyne-Tal, and others) of the "dark ages," so prominently indicate the feasibility with which this Asiatic paradise might be transformed into a flourishing European colony.

Those who know the Himalaya best, will readily admit that numerous localities in the interior of that vast unreclaimed region are by soil, water, and climate admirably suited for English settlements; and as it is proverbial that if Englishmen have a will to penetrate and explore a trackless wilderness, they can generally find a way, it seems almost incredible that after so great a lapse of time, embracing over a century, no serious attempt has yet been made to rear even what may be called a miniature colony in the susceptible heart of this beautiful mountainous tract, and its countless fair valleys, with delightful atmospheric conditions, peaceful and soothing surroundings, sweet sparkling streams, and ever-echoing cataracts, clear and brilliant as diamonds. Here, too, in and along these fresh and charming valleys, melodious with the songs of beautiful birds, the various forests contain innumerable handsome and gigantic trees of many English species, such as the oak, chestnut, pine, birch, etc.; and among those of native growth I will mention only the superb Magnolia as really the Queen of the Forest, when in her spring toilet and crowned with the lovely bloom that scents the air with its honeyed fragrance. Then again, conspicuous among the indigenous fruit trees, are the cherry, walnut, fig, medlar, etc.— not to exclude such modest dainties as raspberries, strawberries, nuts, etc. all growing literally wild. As to the infinite varieties of the fern and flora, my feeble pen would droop in attempting to portray their rare and surpassing beauty—unfading beauty, ever lovable, yet never admired; ever blooming, yet never seen, except by the wild beasts and birds that hold sway over the neglected tracts of which I have here drawn a brief and rough sketch. But there can be little doubt that, in years to come, colonisation will stretch its enterprising arms over these magnificent mountains, to the advantage of England's prestige, in spreading her civilising influence among the semi-barbarous and heterogeneous people (and their name is legion), inhabiting the border-lands, and mysterious unknown countries stretching away from the Great Himalaya Chain into remote and Central Asia.

But I have said enough, and to spare, on this obviously prolific subject, and reluctantly leave it as irrelevant to the narrative in hand. Before doing so, however, I will add that the intelligent reader will easily understand that the writer has been briefly speaking of the Terai and of its occupants, and also of the glorious Himalaya (some of the remotest parts of which he has trodden, where even to the present day no other "white man's stride" has reached), from experience gained, during many sporting tours, and adventurous wanderings over their wildest tracts, in happy days long gone by.

Soon after crossing the Kose, we reached the encampment

of a small European force with which we were to co-operate. And here, our jaded horses having been attended to, we disencumbered ourselves of arms and accoutrements for the first time since our flying march began, and stretching down at rest beneath the shadows of lofty trees, we slept in bundles of straw, coiled up like hedgehogs, with that unbroken soundness familiar to health and fatigue.

CHAPTER 5

The Ghurkas

Thus far it seemed as if these mutineers to whom we were indebted for our late trials—were caught in a fatal trap. For here they were surrounded and intercepted by the Terai, the Kose, and a force of European troops; and: moreover, as the friendly relationship between the Government of India and Nipal appeared true and genuine, we naturally concluded that the Nipalese themselves would readily help us to clear this part of the country—adjoining their own—of the cut-throats who had taken shelter in it, and we also anticipated no delay or difficulty in accomplishing this object; but how far, and with what results, these anticipations were realised will be seen by-and-bye.

That the mutineers had not crossed the river, was a fact known to us all; but the actual locality of their bivouac no one knew-not even the Nipalese inhabitants of the surrounding villages! And yet, they were busy in circulating rumours to the effect that the villains, apprehending certain death from jungle fever by lingering in the Terai, had risked the passage of the river in the darkness of night, and had thus succeeded in getting away!

Needless to say, a deaf ear was turned to these suspicious rumours, and without much ado, we at once started on a farcical search of hide-and-seek along the outskirts of the jungles; and presently found ourselves floundering in treacherous quicksands which were terribly dangerous; so much so indeed that the local guides, who were slowly and cautiously directing our course, informed us that even elephants would not escape being swallowed up bodily, if they ventured over some of them.

Really, our adventurous ride across these quick-sands, though it may not have been a military spectacle of an imposing kind, in the equestrian art it certainly presented a very laughable scene; and the climax in the comical performance was reached, when suddenly we were compelled to hold on like "grim death" to frantic horses plunging, rearing, struggling, wriggling, in short performing a sort of romping "Sir Roger de Coverley," or a fantastic rocking-horse dance, in their nondescript efforts to get through these frightful sands. At length, however, we passed out of them, and found ourselves on the margin of a boundless ocean of bushes and brushwood foliage; but the sun was then setting, and it being too late, especially in a trackless wilderness like this, to proceed farther that day, we bivouacked for the night, and tried to forget our "roughing" to use an impressive phraseology of the corps in repose. But the weather was bitterly cold, in fact the temperature was at freezing point, and the gnawing wind that moaned through the surrounding trees wafted slumber away.

In the absence of clothing it was found impossible to sleep; and all around the bivouac the horses kept up a restless stamp and tramp, while deep and discordant growls issued from the men, as if from the bowels of the earth, on every side. Our only comfort therefore was the fire—kindled by the "guides" to scare away, as they said, the beasts of prey. Towards midnight, while we still sat smoking and basking over the fire, and a sepulchral stillness reigned over the jungles—interrupted occasionally by the loud and dismal howl of jackals—we heard sounds far more impressive and striking than had yet fallen on our ears, sounds as of shouts of exultation long and loud, and savage yells sharp and clear pervading the surrounding gloom. With bated breath and necks craned we listened, while the sentinels called out to one another, and confirmed to each other what had been heard. What were those sounds? whence did they come? could the mutineers be in our vicinity or on the move? were questions earnestly asked, and subsequently answered by a grim apparition in the jungles.

At break of day, after passing a wretched and sleepless night, we pioneered our way along a web of thorny bushes that stretched from the Terai into the plains on all sides, and in solemn silence rode on, backwards and forwards, now here, now there, according to the directions of the "guides"; until at last, a few days having passed in this "wild-goose chase"—this jungly promenade—all hopes of discovering the rebel camp were abandoned; and therefore, for the last time, as the insects began to hum the decline of day and gloom gathered around, we halted for the night in this wild solitude.

Dawn broke obscurely through a mist that did not disperse until noon, and then our retrograde "goose-step" movement towards the plains began; and presently we were gladdened by seeing the open country again, with much the same feeling as castaway mariners are wont to enjoy when in sight of land once more.

But what was to be done next? To abandon the search altogether in uncertainty would doubtless stimulate the panic in the districts where its symptoms had already appeared. Sinister rumours gained ground; alarm spread abroad; a body of revolted troops was known to be "somewhere" in the neighbourhood, and unless their locality was traced out, or their mysterious disappearance accounted for, the departure of the column from so inhospitable a region could not be sanctioned. At all events, that being the "order" of the day, a second search, with the aid, of Nipal Gurkhas , instead of us, immediately commenced.

While the adventurous hunt on the outer fringe of jungles was going on, time with ourselves, now bivouacked in Nipal territory, passed in vigilant monotony, and without any affair of moment occurring. In these inactive moments, therefore, I subjoin a few remarks concerning the Nipal troops, called Gurkhas—with whom we are now in confederate intercourse, and with whom I was well acquainted in days prior to those at present under notice—premising, however, that these scraps, disengaged from all trammels of prejudice and thrown together in the following paragraphs, are intended for the sake merely of readers unacquainted with the "Highlanders" of Nipal.

In the first place, then, it is permissible to say that real Gurkhas are *raræ aves* out of Nipal, and a race by themselves; so much so indeed that if they should ever have occasion to leave their country, it is never for any length of time. True, the Government of India has several so-called Gurkha regiments in its service; but the men of those regiments, though excellent soldiers, are not Gurkhas , but belong to the numerous tribes of the Himalaya, and not to the *Khas*, or real Gurkha race.

They are eminently cheerful, good-tempered, free from prejudice to Europeans; and, though short- statured, are a thickset, broad-shouldered, and large-limbed race of men, with features rarely prepossessing. Their predominant vices are licentiousness, avarice, cruelty, and treachery; their virtues hardihood, patience of fatigue, patriotism, and love of liberty. Their affection for Mammon is as intensely ardent as that of their Hindu neighbours. But they shun as much as possible mercantile pursuits; for, according to their social ideas of trade, a trader holds a peculiar position, in so much that should he become rich he is called a knave, if he continues poor he is deemed a fool! In fact, to reveal their sentiments in this matter clearly, they regard all traders as no better than plausible rogues!

They are blessed with what in common phraseology would be termed "iron constitutions," rarely, if ever, seem sick or sorry, have no experience of medicine, and, as a matter of fact, it would be impossible to find a healthier race in Asia, or discover a more pre-eminently jovial set of fellows than they are. And they possess an amount of rational "chaff" during convivial feasts very seldom, if ever, to be found among people so completely isolated and secluded from foreign intercourse as they always have been; and this is all the more striking, when at such feasts and annual festivals they become strenuous worshippers of Bacchus, and when it is by no means exceptionally rare for these martial spirits to drink off at a draught, or gulp down, full "tumblers" (called *kuttoras*) of some form of alcohol, stronger than raw rum, as if the liquor were water!

In addition to their military equipments, they carry (as may be said of the whole nation) the ancient weapon of Nipal namely, the terrible *kokre*, which, parenthetically described, is a massive curved knife some twenty inches long and about five broad, manufactured from the finest-tempered steel, and whetted with an edge as sharp as that of a razor. The reader, who may not have seen the *kokre* used, cannot by mere description form any conception of its power in the hands of a strong man skilful in the art of wielding it. Even we ourselves, while looking on at some Nipalese sacrificing animals to their gods, could hardly believe our eyes when we saw the head of a buffalo severed from the neck by a single stroke from this truly formidable weapon. The man who performed this amazing feat informed us, with broad grins following a convulsive "Ha, ha!" that he could as easily decapitate two human heads with one blow; and a confederate bystander explained the purport of this savage remark by observing that, in divorce cases, not the ordinary law of civilisation, but the all-powerful *kokre*, summarily settles, and effectually avenges any injury to the matrimonial bed.

A more useful weapon it would be impossible to place in the hands of any man than the *kokre* is in those of the Nipale. He uses it for all purposes, and without it he seldom stirs out abroad. It is his sword, his table-knife, his razor, and his nail-parer; with it he clears the jungle for his cultivation, builds his log-hut, skins the animals that he slaughters—in short, without the *kokre* he is as helpless as a child; with it he is a formidable warrior, as well as a man of all work.

A few days have passed; the season of Christmas-tide approached, and time, as it went on, revealed indications in a manner not to be mistaken, and into which it was not difficult to see, that our worthy "allies" had been engaged in other plans than those which appeared upon the surface; for by this time it had become self-evident that they had been watching, and waiting for a favourable opportunity to throw off the hypocritical mask, in which they had so long performed a deceitful farce; and now that, by the co-operation of their own troops with ours, they conceived their part plausibly played out, with a coolness and nonchalance characteristic of their race, they unanimously proclaimed the escape of the rebels, and in confirmation of their statement voluntarily offered to point out the deserted rebel lair! Of course this unexpected and doubtful news at once aroused an excitement and commotion that soon culminated in a general rush of armed men to the indicated spot, where were found proofs of a recent encampment, and a few dead horses corroborative of the news.

It is needless to describe the rage and indignation that prevailed in the camp, when it was discovered that every man in the expedition had been fooled and duped to hunt for rebels who had already crossed the Kose, and fled during that night when those loud and protracted shouts were heard in the jungles; and so, it will suffice to say, this jungly melodrama, in the end, confirmed the suspicions that had rested on our "allies" as to their having been "charmed" by the plundered treasure of the mutineers, and thus—shall I say it?—that "golden wand" wafted them into thin air!

We were now off on another flying march, and for days together literally lived in the saddle, and rode until our horses were fagged well-nigh to death. But this sweeping and rattling ride—dogging the trail of the fugitives—had the desired effect in pacifying apprehension among the European community of the neighbouring districts, and restoring confidence in a part of the country where alarm, bordering on panic, had already begun to exhibit itself uncomfortably.

Christmas in the Mutiny!

When did Englishmen ever pass a more extraordinary Christmas Day than we did in 1857?

Bivouacked by the roadside in a lovely country surrounded with evergreen foliage, like the holly, decorating the scene, we rested in a, headlong pursuit under wreaths formed of sabres hanging in the trees over our heads like the mistletoe, and thought of all the dear ones in Old England at home, and toast-

ed them in copious draughts of warm milk, while we feasted
ourselves on the only food procurable namely, parched grain,
and some native fruit!

CHAPTER 6

The Murder Site

The mutineers having vanished, we turned our faces to the westward, and marched by comparatively easy stages through Tirhoot; and as we journeyed on from day to day in this district, we found it more attractive in pleasant scenery than any we had yet traversed. True, the general aspect of the landscape was monotonous; but where, it may be asked, on the plains of Upper India is the landscape not monotonous? You might travel thousands of miles, and yet the boundless plains, with almost unvarying rural features, would meet your gaze everywhere. You might look in every direction for miles and miles along the scene for some rare or novel object to break the interminable monotony of the vast outstretching country, but you would look in vain.

Whichever way you may twist or turn, the clustering villages of the peasantry; the hamlet homestead, with its sugar or oil mills; the irrigation wells dotting the fields; the evergreen groves (topes) of mango, tamarind, and other fruit, or ordinary tropical trees; the ruined buildings of ancient times; the Hindu or Mahommedan temples or mosques; now and again rivers, or cities, or towns, or relics of bygone ages, mingle in the picture; and so on and on, miles succeed miles in wonderful and measureless panoramic monotony of rural beauty, which gives the general aspect of the country a look as if it had been cast in the same beautiful mould, and spread out over the land by the same artistic hand. But in contrast to this uniformity of the scenery that of Tirhoot is exceptionally superior in versatility; and is all the more enhanced by a succession of attractive residences scattered over the district amidst picturesque grounds, where extensive factories, and thousands of highly cultivated acres of indigo, mark the industry and prosperity of the Planters. The hospitality, too, for which the Planters in India have always been famed, we found still prevailing unimpaired in this part of the country, and our march through it to Mozufferpur was one of hilarious enjoyment.

As Mozufferpur was the *sudder*, or chief town in Tirhoot, we halted there for a few days, in order to rest the horses and baggage animals for the work on the contemplated line of march. In the place itself there was little worthy of remark, except that it had escaped the deplorable scenes and general calamities of the evil times, and looked pleasant and invited repose.

Our "gala days" as they were termed at Mozufferpur were often recalled to memory with positive ecstasy, when contrasting them with the gloomy ones we subsequently experienced. It was New Year's time, the season of general holiday, the first we had had since our hard work began, and we took advantage of it to enjoy a downright "jolly" halt at this delightful station, until in weather that had set in wet we moved to Motehare.

It rained incessantly, and to journey in a saturated skin is at all times far from agreeable; indeed, few hardships to cavalry can be more intolerable than the discomfort attending long marches over flooded roads and through torrents of rain—no condition more dismal and annoying than that of campaigning life in such inclement weather. We toiled away on the surface of immense submerged plains, and in due course arrived at Motehare, which small station we found deserted by the European community, though it appeared untouched by the remorseless hands of rebels.

While on the march, I pause again for a moment at another little station named Segowle, to note the story of a tragedy in which the actors were the demoniac troopers of a cavalry regiment. It was the only corps stationed at this insignificant cantonment, and so isolated was its position that it seemed beyond the reach of fanatical emissaries or seditious proclamations. Besides, we were told that the Commandant of the regiment never ceased to believe in the loyalty of his men, and over and over again declared them "staunch," and proof against treachery swerving them from their allegiance to the Government.

Sad, therefore, it is to relate that he was murdered in cold blood by these very men whom he had thus extolled. Morbid and infatuated confidence, however, led numerous officers of the Bengal Army to similarly trust bloodthirsty traitors at the commencement of the Mutiny; and they lost their lives in consequence. But, after all, it is not conjectural to say, this "infatuated confidence" originated from ignorance of the inborn Asiatic deceit, and honeyed lies, which are ever hidden under the smooth language and manners of Orientals, and by which many Englishmen—though they may have lived in India among the natives for years—are so easily deceived.

It was with no reluctance that we passed on from this sad and silent cantonment, and in spite of frightful roads, rendered in places almost impassable by the recent rains, entered the Bitteah *raj*. And here, to relieve the dryness of antecedent details, I may remark in passing that late in the evening of our arrival in the town, we were not a little surprised to hear the tolling of the "vesper bell"; and yet not a single European was living in the place, nor even in its neighbourhood.

We were, however, told that Bitteah contained a substantially built Roman Catholic chapel in thorough repair, and that the appurtenances of every description appropriated to the uses of the religion were in perfect preservation. Hence it would seem an interesting question to ask how this Papal sanctuary, situated as it was in the very port-hole of the rebellion, escaped destruction or desecration, when elsewhere the rebels destroyed or defiled all Christian churches and chapels.

However, as the chapel at Bitteah happened to be in a town that belonged to one of the honourable feudal lords, or Barons of Bengal, and not to the rapacious East India Company, it seemed self-evident that only for this reason it was spared. But I am wandering beyond our line of march, and from the Gunduk river, which flows calmly through extremely fertile country, and separates Bengal Proper from the North-West Provinces.

CHAPTER 7

The Perilous Post

Hardly an incident showing an insurrectionary temper in the people, occurred while our route lay through Bengal Proper; but no sooner had we crossed the quiet Gunduk, and invaded the Gorukpur district, where martial law had been proclaimed, than the hostile disposition of the inhabitants began to make itself manifest without the slightest disguise.

The sudden mortality among our horses and beasts of burden inspired us with misgivings that they were falling a sacrifice to poison; but as cattle-poisoning with arsenic, for the sake of the hides, is followed by low-caste curriers as a professional calling in many parts of India, this mortality may not, perhaps, have been occasioned by feelings of hostility among the people with whom our acquaintance had only just commenced. To allay our suspicions, however, the carcases of all animals that died in camp, were always sabred and slashed into ribbons prior to our changing ground.

The *budmashes* (vagabonds), too, were "up and doing," and with such daring boldness were they at work that some were actually seized in broad daylight freebooting in disguise on the outskirts of the camp.

Now, as we carried "the law" in our own free hands, and had almost entirely thrown off the restraints of civilisation, they were without ceremony lashed to trees, and thrashed with a severity that in other times would have been far from gratifying to witness. Still, it must be confessed that, for correcting native vagabonds in the most effectual way during those days, there was nothing like the application of unrelenting rods of iron.

While passing rapidly through the Gorukpur station, we were unable to notice the full extent of the dismal wreck the rebels had left behind them. But, as we rode along, the loyal inhabitants of the town informed us that, immediately the Europeans abandoned the station, their houses were occupied by the rebel usurper—Mahomed Husain—and his followers; that the Christian church and cemetery had been desecrated, and that the whole neighbourhood at once became a huge den of iniquity and vice.

As we advanced, the signs of anarchy became more prominently defined. Fortifications, or rather loop- holed earthworks, erected here and there, forcibly illustrated systematised rebellion; while the people began to put on a more insolent air.

Wild rumours, too, were busy concerning the usurper of the Gorukpur district, who, it was stated, had proclaimed a *jehad* (Crusade, or Holy War) against all Europeans invading his district! Neither was the intelligence received from the Oudh frontier cheering; and among other evil tidings that got spread abroad it was reported: that the territory adjacent to the river Ghagra swarmed with insurgents, and that the very position to which we were proceeding was not free from them. Nevertheless, discrediting these rumours, onward we pressed; and as within thirty miles or so in front of our right flank a Nipalese "ally" army, many thousands strong, was moving on towards Luknow, we did not anticipate experiencing annoyance, or interruption, on the line of our march through this hostile and dangerous section of the country.

I have already stated that in these flying marches the trees stood duty for tents; and as we had now arrived at a large tope wherein some masonry wells marked a halting stage, we bivouacked, and made preparations for passing the night there.

Hard by this bivouac, suspended in the *tope*, we saw for the first time the fruits of retributive punishment in the corpses of rebels dangling from many branches of the trees, and recording the vengeance of some advanced British force, which had left in its trail these ghastly memorials of stern retribution. Some of the bodies encased in gorgeous apparel hung so close to the ground that the limbs to the knees had been eaten away by pariah dogs and jackals; while the upper portions, literally "alive" through decomposition, tainted the very atmosphere of the surrounding neighbourhood. A more revolting spectacle it would be difficult to imagine; and we were only too glad when the hour arrived for us to leave these fetid fames and hideous relics of horror, and respond to the braying of trumpets rousing the Corps to march on again.

Our next halting ground was in the town of Buste; where the inhabitants—though with disguised sycophancy they pretended to be pleased with our arrival—could not hide from us their hostile looks, which seemed to express the truth that we were not welcome.

The only animals for the conveyance of the baggage now being elephants, they were left to follow us leisurely, while we made a long, rattling march to Amorah; and on our way, as we passed through a large village named Cuptangung, it was noticed that a portion of it was fortified, in order to overawe the surrounding country, as well as to facilitate communication with our advanced posts.

In this village several officers of a native infantry regiment perished. Poor fellows! they were decoyed while endeavouring to escape the brutal Sepoys, and cruelly murdered. What the living men had suffered while being hunted down can never be known—except this: that exhausted, foot-sore, wounded, and bleeding, they were slain by the savage foe with demoniac barbarity, as we ascertained on the spot. I mention this cruel tragedy here, merely to show how distressed and distracted our unfortunate countrymen were in the Mutiny days. Not knowing what to do, or whither to fly like ensnared birds awaiting their doom but flying at length for their lives, they actually flew into the very jaws of death.

We did not loiter here, but were soon again jogging along

through a dismal scene, from which all life and animation seemed almost wholly absent; and as we rode on, sometimes across enormous tracts of open country, sometimes in and out of gigantic topes and deserted villages, only a few gaping peasants, or the lowing of stray cattle relieved the dreary aspect and ominous stillness—deepened rather than broken by the monotonous tramp of our horses' hoofs.

But the severest toil, in whatever form, has an end, like everything else. And so this long, weary march ended at length at the village of Amorah; too late, however, after nightfall for us to do more than bivouac in open fields, and rest there on generous earth, with a star-lit, sympathising, cloudless sky above us all.

At Amorah we burst into the full blaze and storm of the rebellion, and found ourselves, after many mouths of unceasing marches, counter-marches, and flying marches, covering an extent of country which in length of mileage would have embraced European kingdoms, suddenly halted for unexplained reasons, and an unknown period.

Although our harassing marches now closed, the circumstance was a disappointment to the corps, and considered by no means satisfactory; for having at last reached, to use a hackneyed phrase, within measurable distance of Luknow (where preparations for the recapture of that important city were in progress), we all felt impatient for removal to those more stirring quarters. Subsequent events, however, following as they did one after another in quick succession, amply justified the peremptory orders that detained us at Amorah. For to have left the position we now held, would undoubtedly have resulted in again abandoning the surrounding country to the rebels; for notwithstanding they had been attacked and driven out of the district, they were still in the neighbourhood, and the sullen booming of their morning, noon, and evening guns afforded the means of ascertaining the direction of their whereabouts—a few miles away at Belwa, and *tête-à-tête*, as it were, with ourselves.

Our position now, with its overpowering sense of loneliness, was not an enviable one; for here we were thrown out on the confines of Oudh, isolated and beyond the support of any force, menaced from Belwa in front by the usurper's insurgents, and from Nugger in rear by a body of mutineers, having to turn out daily for some real or threatened attack, watchworn and jaded with incessant duty, and the apparent impossibility of succour reaching us in time to overawe the rebels—who would have envied such a position? It was an anxious time; but there was no falling off in the confidence of the "B.Y.C."—to use the initials of the corps' designation, as invariably used amongst ourselves. And so from day to day, with bull-dog pertinacity and clenched teeth, we held on to the position, and bore up against the perils that beset us; never thinking we could do so, but we never know how much we can do or bear till we have done or borne it. All of us knew that every man in the corps carried his life in his hand, that he was under the shadow of death, and that his safety, for some time at least, must depend upon his own vigilance and exertions; and the vigilance and exertions of patrols, pickets, sentries, and even of the camp followers never flagged for a moment. In fact, every man in the camp, whether sick or sorry, was permanently on "sentry go" day after day, and night after night.

This prominent allusion to so critical a state of affairs is, I assure you, reader, unalloyed with *braggadocio*, and the Government record (that is to say, the date of the *Gazette*), relating to the dangerous isolation of the corps at this period, is inserted elsewhere in this narrative, and that document will show the forlorn and perilous position into which we had helplessly drifted—a position infested with mutineers, and where every native (the unfortunate peasantry having fled from their homes) was an enemy, or prepared to become such on the first symptoms of wavering on our part. In truth, the surrounding country was surging with revolt; treachery and death lurked on every side; and if we had shown any signs of retreat, or suffered ourselves to be forced from Amorah, the rebels would have been free to overrun the district once more, and carry fire and sword whithersoever they pleased.

Looking back over the whole course of our difficulties, I

conscientiously say without any vain boasting that nothing during the campaign, not even the desperate ordeals through which we subsequently passed, tried our dogged tenacity, and unflinching endurance, more than the unceasing duty at that perilous and important post.

CHAPTER 8

The Journal

Having undertaken to faithfully trace this narrative exactly as it was recorded in the journal of my youth, I have accordingly now to transcribe a few pages of it in diary form, and as this diary records the passing events that actually occurred until we were succoured, its contents will, in some measure, tend to illustrate the perilous position held at this time by the corps.

Amorah, *February 23rd,* 1858.—Early this morning some attention was paid to "comfort," and the tents were pitched in a manner quite novel to witness, and with a tidiness we had not yet seen.

The regimental guards are stationed in front of the encampment, and pickets with chains of *videttes* keep sharp eyes on the surrounding country.

The horses are picketed in four parallel lines of one troop each, and the baggage elephants occupy a patch of ground immediately in rear of the encampment.

The camp followers seeing these unusual precautions taken for the protection of the camp, and hearing the enemy's guns in the distance, begin to show signs of apprehension, so much so that in all probability, if in the darkness of night a hearty cheer was raised by ourselves, few, or perhaps none, of them would be found by daylight to ridicule their fears.

No attempt made to annoy us.

24th.—Duty! duty! everlasting duty continues, and in consequence some grumbling may be excused until the arrival of the Field Force on its way to succour us.

25th.—Last night, without intermission, half the Corps patrolled to and fro in all directions, especially along the main road leading into Oudh grim work! As rebel horsemen were hovering about, fifty sabres were kept in the saddle by day and by night, ready for any emergency.

26th.—This morning a strong patrol, while reconnoitring, intercepted a band of rebels, gave chase, overtook, encountered, and slew some of them; but owing to the difficult ground the rest escaped, except three who were captured, and on their arrival in the camp some sensation was caused when their arms and accoutrements proved them to be genuine Sepoys of the Bengal Army.

As no intelligence concerning the rebels at Belwa could be extracted from them, and to all our interrogatories they assumed a sullen silence, they were at once led away to be hanged; and then followed a scene that, thank God! never—except in such times as these—falls to the lot of Christians to witness. Nobody in the camp who saw that scene has forgotten it, I am sure, or ever will forget it. Within the boundary of the encampment a gibbet having been extemporised in a cluster of trees, the mutineers were ordered to mount the elephant usually employed on such ghastly occasions; this they did with alacrity, and their arms being unpinioned they helped to adjust the nooses in the cords round their own necks; then the elephant by "command" of its keeper moved off, and left the trio suspended to the branches in dying agony, until death—by strangulation—relieved their sufferings.

In ordinary times such scenes would have chilled the blood of the living, but now men who had never perhaps in the whole course of their lives witnessed the execution of a human being were actually superintending, with a sort of superhuman calmness, the "surroundings" of a common hangman. Such, alas! is the eventful epoch we live in, and in which there is no alternative.

27th.—Weather charming; the air mild, the sky clear, and of the loveliest turquoise blue Mars and Ceres appear in strange fellowship at Amorah. A boundless and rolling carpet of rich crops lies spread out before us on every side, but not a living form is seen lingering about the pleasant landscape. Heavy firing at intervals on the Oudh frontier. Every horse saddled; every man accoutred and on the alert. Sent off a spy to the rebel camp at Belwa. He is, I am told, a desperate scoundrel; but as at the risk of his life he proved himself faithful to us on a former occasion, he was again allowed to venture into the enemy's lines.

As I sit conversing with a churn under the protruding outer fly of our tent, overlooking the main road, one of the pickets is seen galloping in at speed. We feel conscious of something unusual having occurred. He sweeps round to the commandant's quarters, and now we hear the "assembly"; we fly to the horses.

28th.—The "alarm" was a true one. The picket, surprised by the approach of some rebels, called in the videttes, formed up, despatched a messenger to the camp, then charged and engaged the ruffians in a hand-to-hand encounter. But not yet had the notes of the trumpets ceased when the camp-picket of fifty sabres were let loose, and away they rushed "to the rescue," while the main body to a man stood with bridle in hand if need be in readiness to mount. The picket had, however, attacked with such vigour and effect that, before aid could reach our fellows, the rebels were routed, and thrown out in their calculations; for, armed with muskets and matchlocks, which commanded a longer range than our carbines and revolvers, they probably had calculated on driving in the outposts, with a view no doubt to ascertaining our strength. Thus warned, as it were, we passed the night fully accoutred and on the *qui vive*.

In yesterday's affair several of the picket were wounded, but poor Randolph was killed. His head was literally cloven in two by a sword cut, and over the shoulder there was a wound extending right down into the lungs. Early in the morning his remains, wrapped in a horse-cloth, were buried, while the perpetual booming of the enemy's guns in the distance, formed an appropriate accompaniment to the short prayer read over his grave, by the lieutenant of the troop to which he belonged.

Being the first volunteer killed in action, Randolph's name is recorded here; but no other casualty in the Corps will be mentioned in this narrative, for the melancholy list, alas! is too long, to warrant its insertion within the narrow space allotted to these pages. I may, however, mention that the numerous *Government Gazettes* of 1858, and 1859, contain the category of the killed and wounded.

March 1st. Although the safety of our position is reduced to a calculation of hours, and our heads are in tigers' mouths, it was cheering to hear that the advance guard of the Field Force would be with us on the morrow. From the rebel camp the spy also brought intelligence of armed men flocking out of the Belwa fort, and preparing for a foraging raid over the district. And to this information he also supplemented other intimations concerning the movements of the rebels, which, as on a former occasion, proved so true that, instead of being a "desperate scoundrel" as his fellow camp followers for some occult reason had dubbed him he became the native hero in the camp; and when the fighting commenced in downright earnest, he was present in all the engagements, sticking to the corps like a leech, until eventually the brave fellow, with broken sword in hand, was killed while endeavouring to save the life of a wounded trooper. Such was the fate of Mohun (a low-caste shoemaker), than whom a more faithful, and courageous spy no European force ever had in India.

The purport of the message received from the Field Force was, of course, known only to those in command of the corps, but immediately on its receipt we were warned to march as soon as there should be daylight enough, for obvious reasons, to discern objects at considerable distances. As to the camp, that was to be left standing under the protection of the approaching advance guard; while the camp followers were instructed to await the arrival of the whole force before striking the tents, and with baggage, etc., following the road we were about to take.

When the morning brightened, we drew sabres and moved off into an unpleasant white mist that hung over our route, but it did not last long before the rising sun, and as it disappeared the features of the country towards which we were proceeding could be distinctly traced for miles in their forlorn solitude- even the very villages we passed were wholly deserted. But this dull, monotonous ride was suddenly enlivened on our reaching some undulating land in the environs of Belwa, and coming in view of its swarming insurgents.

And here we had hardly halted, when round-shot ploughed across the fields and ricocheted over the slopes that protected us, while shells rushed and hissed like monsters of the air above our devoted heads—the heads only were visible from the fort, so that the instant the smoke of the cannon appeared in the embrasures, they bobbed approval as regularly and simultaneously as if they had moved by machinery. The rebel sharpshooters, too, appeared active, for as we looked up at them we could see hundreds more venturesome than others sally out rifle in hand, advance some distance in front, and with long, sustained aim, fire. They were, however, indifferent marksmen, inasmuch as, with the exception of a few bullets whizzing harmlessly past our ears, all their shots fell short.

A bird's-eye glance having been cast over the fortress and its environs, amid savage yells mingled with foul execrations poured out upon us by the villains, we retraced our steps to Amorah; and about halfway between that village and the rebel stronghold just reconnoitred, we met our camp equipage and followers *en route* to join us. And this circumstance was exhilarating to all spirits; it was in fact, as it were, the "friendly precursor" of the Field Force, and indicated the arrival of succour within hailing distance at last so that whatever might now follow, incidental to the recent passage-of-arms before the fort, we had its support, as well as our own good sabres to trust to.

A word here about Belwa may not be without some interest to the reader, though I sketch the features of the whole place merely in outline; for living as we were in the saddle, with graves always open at our feet, and grappling with a rebellion in which human blood was flowing like water, we were in no mood to notice in detail the general aspect of any place or scenery.

Belwa, then; is a village situated on the confines of the Goruk-pur district, and overlooks the river Ghagra, which flows between it and Ajudya, the ancient capital city of Oudh. The plains on which this village lies, and through which this boundary river passes, are remarkably fertile, but in rural features without any pretensions to landscape beauty. Across these plains runs the high road to Luknow, and to the right of them extensive fields stretch onwards until they vanish from sight near the banks of the Ghagra on the one side, and likewise disappear in a vast circular sweep of vegetation on the other. In the background *topes* form a sort of amphitheatre on a colossal scale, and in front of all is the plateau on which the village of Belwa stands; while in a sandy dip adjoining this plateau its fort frowns over the surrounding country.

This village and fort, as well as other adjacent earthworks, were occupied by Nipal troops when we reached Amorah; but the day following our arrival, they suddenly evacuated the place, and started to rejoin their chief (Jung Bahadur), who was then with a Nipalese army on the march to Luknow. And to this extraordinary "move" must be attributed the harassing trouble and toil through which we struggled.

The insurgents were well aware of the importance of this formidable post, considerably increased by the difficult nature of the ground, possessing the command of the highway into Oudh, and having all the advantages of a concentric position; they were therefore not slow in seizing it immediately after the Nipalese had retired.

On the spot where we met our camp-equipage the corps rested *en bivouac*, and was there presently joined by the Field Force. With the union, we enter upon a new stage in our eventful career, as the next chapter will show.

CHAPTER 9

The Assault

Our bivouac presented an animated, and rather a singular scene, by the appearance upon the stage of the troops destined to act a prominent part in the approaching struggles.

Groups of England's "hearts of oak," seated on the backs of horses harnessed to naval guns, here represented Jack Tar literally as the proverbial "Horse Marine." Knots of those splendid amphibious bulldogs, the Royal Marine Light Infantry, stood among us and related their recent experiences. There was a fine body of Sikhs—fierce, resolute-looking fellows, with an air of military dash about them. And not the least remarkable among this martial and motley assembly, with all its variety of mien and attitude, race and colour, was a very strong (numerically) regiment of Gurkhas.

Although we are now to co-operate with a distinguished Field Force—which for the sake of brevity will in future be termed Brigade with its proceedings this narrative will interfere as little as possible. It may, however, be noted here that its total number of all arms was some three thousand men, and of these only ourselves (two hundred and fifty) were cavalry.

In the memorable afternoon of March 2nd, 1858, the Brigade, under the command of Brigadier Rowcroft, set forward to capture the fort of Belwa by *coup de main*; and when we were once fairly on the line of march, the distance to that stronghold seemed as short as the hour in which it was accomplished.

Preparatory to the assault, the disposition of the force was made in a few minutes; and where the ground displayed any advantages for artillery, it was at once occupied. The infantry were drawn up in line, with their flanks covered by the cavalry; while at some distance in front of the village a strong body of Marines and Sikhs, partially protected by a tope from the fire of the rebel batteries, guarded the main road, and at the same time distracted the attention of the besieged.

The enemy during the day had not been idle; for since our reconnaissance in the morning, and anticipating an attack in consequence, he had strengthened himself by calling in to his aid other rebel troops from Oudh. Besides, as indications to the ranges of his guns, he had attached huge bundles of brambles to long bamboos and stuck them into the ground here, there, and everywhere, in front of the cannonading distance of his bastions.

By this time the fortifications were thronged with defenders, who began to pour forth a heavy though an ineffectual fire on our line; and this thundering cannonade was the signal for our guns and shell-rockets to open. Still, though shell and round-shot in rapid succession continued to plough into the walls and curtains of the fort, no breach or any aperture could be discerned in it. But listen to the bugles ringing out the advance, and now see Jack Tar responding to their call by galloping up his guns to a murderous range; and then the bombardment commenced in right good earnest.

Meanwhile the marines and Sikhs, pushing on in skirmishing order, trod down all opposition, gained the outskirts of the village, broke through the resistance offered there, and with a final rush drove out the insurgents at the point of the bayonet. Belwa was won, but not its fort. Though the bombardment continued with unabating fury, no serious impression could be made on the stronghold; and long after dusk, in the hellish glare that now and again burst out from the explosions of the infernal missiles hurled at and from the fort, the rebels were visible lining the ramparts in crowds. Secure within strong defences, and outnumbering the Brigade by at least five to one, they could well afford to display a daring tenacity worthy of the old days, when they so courageously fought on behalf of the East India Company.

Darkness frustrated further efforts; and it was as well that it did so, for it had been amply proved that the strength of the Brigade was altogether insufficient to effect its object. If an attempt had been made to capture the place by storm, a tremendous sacrifice of human life must have occurred; and if the attempt had ended in failure, the consequences would inevitably have been most disastrous to this and the adjoining district of Azimghur. As it was we lost something of the prestige which at first surrounded us, by the ineffectual blow struck at the fort of Belwa.

The attack on the fort having terminated unsuccessfully, the conquered village was evacuated, and the Brigade retired in good order, and by moonlight fell back to the same bivouac, whence it had started in the afternoon with a view to capture the rebel stronghold.

Perceiving the favourable turn affairs had taken in his behalf, and emboldened by temporary success, the enemy did not remain inactive; for not many hours after we had bivouacked, detachments of his infantry were reported to be crossing the Ghagra, and hurrying to Belwa.

There was, therefore, a sort of "council of war," in which good counsels prevailed, inasmuch as they decided our return to Amorah; and by resorting to this retrograde movement, it was suggested that the enemy would probably be encouraged to encounter the Brigade in the field, with the result no doubt of a terrible thrashing overtaking him; besides, it was hoped that in the open country the victory would be not only sure, but decisive, so decisive as to reassure the unfortunate peasantry, who had to a man fled the country.

As Amorah was destined to become the scene of more than one sanguinary action, and fated to obtain considerable celebrity, I will just remark in passing that it is a village very superior to those generally found in that part of the country; and the high road that passed through it may be termed the key-route to the southern districts. In its front were boundless plains dotted with hamlets and fields. On its right a vast stretch of open country commanded the approaches in that direction; while on its left the land was as flat as a pancake, and continued so until at length it disappeared, as it were, to the eye in the distance, as far as the horizon. Such, in brief outline, was the nature of the surrounding country wherein the tents of the Brigade were pitched, and where we awaited the onset of the rebel hordes.

As regards the precautions that were deemed necessary for the protection of the camp, I need only mention that nothing seemed omitted for safeguarding it. Outposts were stationed, pickets outlying and inlying planted, patrolling squads formed; in a word, everything was done to render its critical position safe.

Nothing however occurred until early morn on March 5th, when, as the troops were busy looking to their arms and ammunition, for the eternal bellowing of the enemy's guns had put them considerably upon their mettle, tidings were brought that the rebels were advancing in great force. So that, after all, our retreat from Belwa resulted, as anticipated, in enticing the miscreants to venture an encounter with us in the field; and as they now approached, the Brigade moved out in readiness to welcome them, and formed up for action thus: the guns, well horsed and manned by the bold sons of Neptune (naval warriors of H.M.S. *Pearl*), took ground in the centre; the infantry, forming; strong columns, extended in line on each side of the guns; while the whole of the cavalry, divided into two squadrons, guarded both flanks of the Brigade.

On came the enemy, like swarms of locusts, the serried lines of gleaming bayonets bristling above an extensive belt of brushwood indicating the masses coming up in long succession, and forming behind the vegetation masking their advance. At this juncture any offensive demonstration was impracticable, for they had not yet emerged from under cover; but the suspense was soon cut short by a shell from the naval guns bursting in their midst, and stirring them up for action.

Their advance, by the notes of bugles, was covered by a

sweeping fire from heavy artillery posted on the main road, and a withering discharge of musketry from the surrounding fields, in which the Sepoys swarmed by thousands. And what a strange spectacle it was, to be sure, to see these veteran troops now engaged in a deadly struggle against those with whom, in former days, they had fought side by side in many desperate wars!

In vain the gallant Jack Tars poured torrents of grape into their thronged ranks, before which they went down like ninepins; in spite of the marines showering volley after volley into their advancing columns, and the Sikhs and Gurkhas, shoulder to shoulder, bravely holding their ground, the rebels step by step pressed on. Flushed with temporary success at Belwa, and backed by an immense numerical superiority in men and guns, they had recklessly imagined victory as easily gained in the open field, as with characteristic vanity they claimed one—in a fortress—from which we had prudently retired.

While every man of the Brigade was desperately engaged in beating down the overwhelming obstinacy experienced in front, and the fury of the action had extended to our flanks, alarm was raised that the rebels were outflanking us, and making for the camp. Then in that critical moment a desperate movement was resorted to, which happily resulted, it may be said, in turning the doubtful fortunes of the day.

The cavalry was ordered to pass forward, and charge a surging column of mutineers pushing on to support the centre of their line. Accordingly, the instant the word "charge" was given, the Yeomanry gave the spur to their horses, and encountered a deadly hand-to-hand struggle, which they terminated by annihilating the head of the column.

So far, so good. But the immediate effect of this charge was electrical on the main body; for, hearing with surprise the din of the desperate *mêlée*, they hesitated in their advance, recoiled, then rallied, and in dense, disorderly masses pressed in towards their centre, while the "broken column," disorganised by the charge, likewise collapsed with confusion in the same direction. An opportunity thus occurred for attacking them to advantage, which was not permitted to escape. The brigadier seized on the moment, and charging with the whole force in line burst through everything that opposed him. Meanwhile the exterminating fire of the sailors paved the way for the infantry, as with levelled bayonets they rushed on to the guns. There the conflict raged fiercely, the cold steel doing its murderous work unrelentingly, as evidenced by the jags in our sabre-blades retaining pieces of bone, and blood-besmeared hair.

In thus dealing out this stern retribution, it must not be imagined that in revenge we were thirsting for blood. On the contrary, we were weary of shedding it, God knows. But the reader will bear in mind, that it was "war to the knife," and that if we had shown any mercy to these ferocious scoundrels, they would assuredly have shot us down the next moment. It was a matter of life or death, to kill or be killed; and if we had stayed our hand, we should undoubtedly have courted our own destruction.

At length, unable to sustain the combined assault of a force fighting like enraged tigers, the rebels yielded reluctantly, contesting each position as they abandoned it.

The action closed in the afternoon, and on the Brigade's return to the camp, a salute from the captured guns (nine with ammunition, tumbrels complete) proclaimed to the surrounding country the triumphant victory, which saved the district a second disastrous invasion.

But, although victory after victory continued to follow our arms in succession, the abovementioned salute was our first, and last one during the campaign, for not a grain of powder could be spared subsequently.

And here I subjoin a short extract from Brigadier Rowcroft''s despatch No. 168, and dated March 6th, 1858 (as published in the Government Gazettes), relating to the service rendered by the Corps in the above briefly described action.

I saw there was no time to be lost, and that a rapid and decisive blow must be struck," writes the Brigadier in his official despatch. "I rode on to the cavalry, and ordered it to advance rapidly inclining to the right, and to charge the enemy's *sowars* [1] and infantry, hoping it would shake their centre. The result of this movement was soon apparent. I saw the left of the enemy hesitate, and the sowars in rapid retreat. Down came the Yeomanry at a charging pace, well and steadily together, on the moving masses of infantry, cutting down and killing great numbers, over a hundred reported. The whole left of the enemy soon gave way. I galloped up to the Yeomanry cavalry, and thanked them for their good, gallant movement and charge; and ordered them to move towards the left to threaten the enemy's centre. When ordering the Yeomanry to advance, I detached a party of troopers to the rear of the naval guns to cover and protect them; and this party, by their gallant and excellent service, aided in capturing some of the guns.

This extract speaks for itself, and I need not add a single word of comment.

A remorseless action of some eight hours' duration, deserves more recognition in descriptive detail, than a brief notice of it in the form of a mere epitome, such as that above recorded. But as I was only a volunteer trooper, and not a war correspondent—who always sees more of the fighting than those engaged in it—I have written merely the facts and incidents that came under my own observation. Besides, during those long mortal hours of slaughter, the battle-field at intervals was so shrouded and wrapped up in its own smoke, that a detailed description of it was obviously impossible to note.

Before closing this chapter, however, I am tempted to remark—in no spirit of boasting, but as a mere record of fact—that after the above-recorded tough tussle (when we were deservedly thanked by the brigadier on the field) the rebels were flattering enough to dub the corps by the impolite name of Shitane Pultun, which may be freely rendered in plain English as regiment of devils. And as this unique information was conveyed to us by our faithful spy Mohun, to whom I have already al-

1. Cavalry.

luded in these pages, it was implicitly believed; and that "satanic appellation," needless to say, stuck to the corps until the end of the campaign.

CHAPTER 10

The "Fiery Dragon"

Late in the afternoon succeeding the victory, the European troops, formed into three sides of a hollow square under the peaceful azure sky, witnessed the burial of the killed. And the sad ceremony of the funeral service that was observed over the mortal remains of those fine fellows, who had but just fought and fallen by the side of those now looking on, must have touched every heart there, even were its nature at other times cold and hard as a stone. And doubtless there were many noble fellows of all ranks in that assemblage who, though ordinarily taking little heed of military obsequies, in this last duty due to the honourable slain, whispered a prayer to the gates of Heaven, on behalf of their fallen comrades in arms.

Amidst manifestations of general rejoicing, mingled with sorrow after the action, it was not forgotten that the camp was put in jeopardy by the rebels outflanking the Brigade. Had they boldly precipitated their attempt to capture it, the disastrous consequences would undoubtedly have been the annihilation of the feeble guard, the indiscriminate massacre of our sick and wounded, the helpless flight of the camp followers, the destruction of the magazine and commissariat stores; while the Brigade itself, attacked simultaneously both in front and from the rear by an exasperated foe, would probably have had to retreat with calamitous loss.

To guard against the possibility of such a disaster happening, however, it was decided to encompass the camp with trenches, so as to render it somewhat secure; while for the protection of the hospital and magazine, the erection of earthworks, mounted with the captured guns, and made defensible against everything but regular siege operations, was deemed necessary to meet any emergency that might arise. Accordingly the work of entrenching and fortifying commenced, while all huts or houses that stood in the line of fire were levelled—the baggage elephants being employed in the latter task, instead of sappers, of whom there were none, and very serviceable they proved. Much spirit and steady labour having been thrown into the work, the position soon became defensible, and in consequence considerable saving in watchfulness temporarily followed.

The result of the victory paralysed the rebels; and was productive of so salutary an effect upon the inhabitants of the district that shoals of the peasantry, who in numbers form the most important part of the population, returned to their homes, from which they had fled at the commencement of hostilities. And as therefore a short interval of tranquillity has now to be recorded, I will slightly digress in the course of the narrative, in order to speak of these good and gentle people (among whom it has been my lot to be thrown for years, and with whom I have often had to pass months consecutively, without seeing a white face, or speaking a word of my native tongue), as well as to show the attitude they assumed in the dreadful times of the Mutiny.

It is impossible for those who have not actually lived among the peasantry of Upper India, and who have not themselves had experience of their innate character and of their inner life, to be able fully to realise their amiability of disposition and inborn goodness of heart. They are a people so mild, so docile, so humane, so submissive in deportment, and withal so faithful, that their nature would recoil with horror at any act of cruelty or treachery. They are known to venerate even the very insects of the earth, and regard all animals as having been formed like themselves by the decree of God, whose life they have no more right to take away or to put it to corporal pain wantonly than that of a human being. Moreover, taking them all together, they possess a wonderful similarity of disposition in showing much sympathy and kindness, not alone towards each other when in trouble or distress, but even to perfect strangers. "Live and let live" is their undying maxim, and so rigidly do they adhere to the principle of this sympathetic fellow- feeling, that the most productive lands adjoining their villages are often gratuitously set apart as Bhiya-Chara, which, being interpreted, means provision for the poor Brotherhood. Where in the wide civilised world, it may be asked, will one find more forethought, kindness of heart, and less personal selfishness than this? And yet, the phenomenal fact remains, that the Sepoys who committed the bloodthirsty massacres and murders, were actually recruited from among these very peasantry.

The limits which I have prescribed to myself in these fragmentary pages, prevent my going into a detail of circumstances to prove the above-stated startling fact in this place; but I shall have something to say on the subject, when I come to speak of the cause that led the sepoys to commit such cruel and inhuman atrocities, as positively shocked and horrified their own rustic parents and brethren.

Whatever may have been their natural feelings of indignation raised by the perfidious cry of their caste being on the brink of destruction, these faithful peasantry remained steadfast in their allegiance to the Government that had brought them within the pale of civilisation. And through all the vicissitudes of the Mutiny—through all the horrors of that sanguinary epoch, their sympathies were with the *Sahibs* (European gentry). As a rule, they not only manifested the utmost repugnance to the cause of the rebellion, but fearlessly supported the authorities where they were able to resist the influence of the vortex in which vast numbers were engulfed, like thousands of the sepoys; who were positively the victims of the revolt themselves. The sweets of the East India Company's rule—albeit with all its bitter faults—were not to them untasted. They compared the humiliating oppression to which they were yoked, under a Mahommedan dynasty, and in some measure treated as beasts of burden, to the freedom they had enjoyed within the last century. Impartial justice and kind treatment had mitigated the evils of their former lot; and these reminiscences, comparatively fresh in their minds, were not susceptible of being erased by any sudden change of circumstances that partially successful rebellion might temporarily have brought. Moreover, their traditional memorials indicated the degrading and hopeless bondage, so to speak, through which their forefathers had passed, and which was not likely to be forgotten by a people, whose ancestors were reduced through despotism to a position of abject serfs. Influenced, therefore, by such bitter reminiscences, they could not act otherwise than maintain a staunch adherence to the Government where they were strong, and continue virtually neutral where they were weak. They were, in fact, either passively, or actively, loyal.

No doubt the wealthy, high-caste Hindu could have stirred up, and led away into the raging flood tens of thousands of these rustic peasantry by the influence of his social position, religion, and caste; but knowing as he well did that the Mahommedan was the prime agitator of the struggle for Empire, as well as at the bottom of the Mutiny, and comprehending to the full extent the ambitious character of that population, he firmly abstained from a share in the rebellion, lest, by the re-establishment of pitiless despotism, he should be the greater loser in the end.

That many aggrieved Hindus, and some of them, too, of exalted rank and great wealth, had just cause to deplore the cruel wrongs they had suffered through the "policy" of the East India Company, and in consequence took advantage of the Sepoy revolt by joining the mutineers, nobody denies—no more than that the local peasantry who so eagerly plunged into the rebellion, were those associated in some capacity or other with these wronged Hindu families.

As a mark of gratitude due, therefore, to the great bulk of the Hindu peasantry of Upper India—in which are included those of the Punjab—I am glad to bear tribute to their faithful conduct, and have accordingly recorded their sincere loyalty in these pages. For, considering that the Mutiny developed the most formidable military revolt on record, and produced such a catastrophe as history has never known, had they cast in their lot with their sepoy brethren, and made common cause with them in the revolt—even if only to the extent of cutting off all food supplies—what would have been the fate of India? I will leave those who were in the Empire during those disastrous days to answer so momentous a question, without venturing to proffer my own opinion on the subject.

Resuming the course of the narrative from the above digression, the approach of the "fiery dragon, the scorching ordeal," has to be recorded.

Time rolled on—the torrid season was coming fast, while rich crops ready for the sickle waved in the hot winds then setting in. By degrees the harvest was garnered, and the country shorn of its vegetation wore a dreary aspect. Its genial charm was gone; where bountiful fields had been, there were now bare flat plains. The atmosphere day by day increased to a fiercer heat, and the whole face of the visible earth dazzled the eye that looked upon it. The bracing cold weather, in fact, had been succeeded by the flaming furnace that blazes over Upper India during its "summer" months.

Without the slightest exaggeration, it may be safely said that no one who has not himself had personal experience of the open-air heat of the abovementioned region, can form any conception of its intensity. In the compass of the heavens, without a cloud even as diminutive as a butterfly to screen his blinding rays, the sun appears from day to day, and for months, like an enormous ruby set in a burnished dome of brass, whence descends a fiery glow almost akin to that derivable from the focus of a burning-glass.

There was no thermometer in the camp, but it required no meteorologist to pronounce what the temperature would have registered in the shade about noon; no less than from a hundred and thirty, to a hundred and forty degrees, we were sure. But all Englishmen stimulated by necessity, "the mother of invention," are not dilatory in discovering solutions for their difficulties especially when they are abroad. So we excavated the ground under our tents to a depth of several feet; and in these miserable "underground apartments," or rather living tombs, with reading and writing, cards and pipes, sentimental ditties and comic songs—which were, of course, always encored—to say nothing of spinning endless yarns and telling mirthful stories, we contrived to while away the weary and fiery hours, as pleasantly as rabbits are wont to do in their appropriate warrens. And it was in holes such as these, that I employed myself in writing the journal from which is transcribed this narrative, so far as it relates to our life and operations in the field.

While domiciled in these inhospitable burrows, we were sometimes molested by such unwelcome visitors as the deadly snake called the *karith*—in search of, perhaps, a more agreeable temperature than that of above ground? Yet it seems strange, and it will hardly be believed, but it is nevertheless a fact, that the *karith*, like the cobra, is naturally partial to places where men live. And although this dangerous reptile is only half the size of a cobra, it is equally venomous. A sting from either is certain death in a few hours; and that being indisputably true, it is curious to note that the *karith* and cobra persistently haunt the dwellings of men, whilst the other numerous species of snakes far less poisonous—some indeed harmless—rarely approach human habitations at all. No wonder, then, that thousands and thousands of the rural population year after year die from the fatal bite of the *karith* and cobra, from which recovery has never been known.

At this time, too, yet another fatal foe appeared in these subterranean ovens, in the form of small-pox, which broke out and spread through the camp. Although sickness is ever to be found in the footsteps of war, the frightful nature of this disease could not but be deplored as a terrible calamity by any force pent up, as we were, like worms under earth, and undergoing manifold trials almost beyond belief. What with the camp having become a *lazaretto*, for the very air we breathed must have been heavily laden with infection; what with the misery of existing in disease-tainted holes; the excruciating heat, the suffocating dust, the inconceivable swarms of flies; with fever, dysentery, gangrene sores, all simultaneously prevalent in the camp, the contagious disease was helped but too fatally in finding easy victims among us.

In the midst of these horrors and this gloomy state of things, it may be asked how we fared in respect to commissariat provisions. Well, to tell the truth, it was always sheer hunger that forced us to cram them down our throats. Meat particularly was seldom barely better than carrion itself, and sometimes indeed so uninviting to the appetite and eye that one could hardly look at it without holding one's nose—no facetiousness is here implied—and this, too, be it remembered by all who read this, in times when at any moment our mettle, energy, and biceps were liable to be tested against a desperate and bloodthirsty foe in the field. Smokable tobacco was not procurable for its weight in gold; and as to wine or ale, no such luxury was now even dreamt of—execrable rum diluted with foul tepid water, was the vile and poisonous alcoholic beverage to which all were confined. I could dwell a great while upon the woeful subject contained in this sombre paragraph, but I think I have said enough already, to represent the complicated distress and misery through which we had passed, and were passing during this dreadful time.

Dismal as this melancholy combination of circumstances had rendered our wretched existence, the news of the capture of Luknow threw a cheerful gleam of light over the gloom of despondency that pervaded the camp. Besides, by the fall of that turbulent city, the confidence of the people became so reassured that they voluntarily acted as spies on our behalf in the enemy's lines; while such was the alarm created by that event that, although the rebel force had lately been augmented, they seemed more reluctant than ever to venture beyond the precincts of their stronghold.

Meanwhile the vigilance, zeal, and devotedness of the Brigade never relaxed or flagged for an hour, and the same precautions for its protection as were observed when it first reached Amorah still continued.

It was during this anxious time of unceasing vigilance that the corps had death ever present by its side; for while scouring the surrounding country throughout the night and reconnoitring by moonlight, a close, well-directed volley from any of the deserted villages that lay along the line of roads we patrolled, must inevitably have brought down the whole patrolling party, like a flock of birds as with a single shot. But familiarity with danger breeds contempt for it; though, at the same time, it was a matter for congratulation that the rebels preferred their comfortable sleep within the Belwa fort, to lurking in ambush out of it.

CHAPTER 11

The Charge

We come now to a memorable day—April 17th, 1858—on which the unbroken tranquillity of a brief interval, since our last encounter with the enemy, was disturbed by vigorous cannonading on the Oudh frontier.

Now experience—and experience tends to instruct, and ripen men more than time—had taught us a valuable lesson in the preliminary tactics of rebel warfare; for we had learned that whenever they really meant to attack us, they invariably commenced the prelude to their operations with as much arrogant noise as possible; and as spies had previously brought intelligence of fugitive mutineers from Luknow having fraternised with their friends at Belwa, the prospect of another struggle became evident, and the roar of the hostile thunder as it echoed over the placid plains was greeted cheerfully, and roused the Brigade for the deadly encounter that was coming.

All was now activity and preparation for thrashing the approaching rebel army; and as soon as the troops were under arms, and all things pronounced in order for action, the word was given to advance, and in two contiguous columns the Brigade moved out to the attack.

The rebels came on with all the confidence imparted by superior numerical strength, though their appearance was rather "picturesque" than military, insomuch that from right to left within eye-range they appeared arrayed in a variety of showy costumes, while moving about in their midst were elephants also gaudily caparisoned. The sepoy portion of this host, however, retained what might be termed half of their original uniform- that is to say, they wore the regulation white jacket of their defunct regiments, while their nether garments were strictly native. Their horse artillery (formerly, of course, belonging to the East India Company, but now " annexed" to their own forces) also astonished us by displaying surprising facility of movement; and in spite of the rugged ground that intersected the flat country, they could be distinctly seen galloping at speed from position to position, and bringing their guns to bear upon our ranks with a precision equal to the celerity with which they limbered up and unlimbered, and which was unquestionably worthy of applause.

A general fusillade opened on both sides, and was immediately followed by a thundering cannonade. A sanguinary conflict now ensued, and men began to drop, few killed, many wounded. The clash of arms, the deafening roar of guns, the whizzing of shells and thousands of bullets, all evidenced the desperate onset and fight. But as by this time dense clouds of smoke and dust had enveloped the whole scene, it will, nay, it must, suffice (for, as already stated, I am relating throughout this narrative only what I saw) to say that after repeated efforts to check the Brigade in its crashing advance, the rebels in despair commenced leisurely to retreat.

Presently, however, a gun opening in front of our right flank announced the proximity of another rebel force, and this incident seemed to reassure the retreating multitude, for they faced about, and made further efforts to stand; but in vain. Grape-shot swept them off once more as before; the front ranks broke, those behind recoiled, wild panic and disorderly rout ensued. With increased impetuosity the advance continued, until our line debouching from a *tope*, we saw in the distance a body of sepoys vainly attempting to rally the vanquished fugitives; but terror-stricken the beaten and scattered host heeded them not, and away over the road and fields with active strides, they soon disappeared behind the surrounding woodlands.

In front of the position on which the sepoys, under notice,

had apparently decided to make a final stand, stretched an extensive plain, in the rear was the main road leading into Oudh, on the right the land declined to broad ravines of difficult access, and close by on the left, enfolded in the graceful arms of gigantic trees, reclined a pleasant-looking little village, bearing the soft and gentle name of Tilga—a spot in appearance so picturesque and peaceful, that it seemed unnaturally savage to associate its charming rural precincts with a ghastly and deadly struggle, such as the one that was just on the point of being witnessed.

From our point of view, this body of mutineers seemed so small that, notwithstanding they were supported by a grim eighteen-pounder gun, a squadron of the corps was deemed sufficient to dislodge, if not literally to annihilate them. Accordingly one hundred and twenty-two sabres, with the colonel at their head, prepared to charge. The words march, trot, gallop, in rapid succession, had scarcely passed the lips of the leader, when on dashed the Yeomanry like greyhounds slipped for the chase. They sweep over the plain, they plunge into an intercepting ravine half full of water that momentarily checks their race into the jaws of death, they tear through the stream in the teeth of a shower of grape from the eighteen-pounder.

Still on flew the squadron, with every nerve braced, every sabre gripped; knee to knee the on-rushing wave of steel roared, as it were, "Now for the gun! Now for the gun!" as the scowling black monster from its gaping muzzle vomits for the last time another discharge of deadly grape into our faces; but with free rein, neck and neck, and outstretched strides the maddened and gallant horses fly, like the irresistible shower of the iron hail that had just flown over their heads. Yet the mutineers, with muskets levelled from the shoulder, stand like posts, and draw not a trigger—a few strides more and bayonet and sabre would have crossed each other—when lo! in an instant up sprang hundreds of Sepoys on every side as if out of the very ground itself. They had been crouching, in fact, like tigers prepared to spring from behind the village, and the thin line of their front ranks by which we were decoyed. It was now too late to check the headlong rush, and had it been attempted, in the confusion that doubtless would have followed, the destruction of the whole squadron would probably have been the result. No sooner therefore were these numerous assailants disclosed than the colonel thundered forth, Charge! And the next moment a stream of musketry, like a sheet of fire, met us with terrible effect, and literally cut down a section of the squadron, and encumbered the spot where this withering volley was received, with men and horses struggling in dying agony.

But nothing could daunt the remnant of that devoted band, and seeing their comrades fall, with wild enthusiasm and sabres flashing in the blazing sunshine, they plunged in among the enemy with an ardour that could not be resisted; and then followed a scene which to this day has not faded from the memories of those who saw it—a scene of dare-devil enterprise, which my feeble pen would fail to describe with adequate force, and tragical effect.

In an area of heaven knows how many square yards, the killed and wounded lay crowded together as they had fallen; while some of the latter, having been blown off their horses when within a few yards of the muskets, with their "garments" yes, reader, garments (for many of us, in contempt for dress, were fighting in shirt sleeves)—on fire, were unable to move; others fell and died without a groan; others, weltering in their blood, or bleeding to death, dragged themselves up into sitting postures, and with revolvers in hand watched the doubtful fight; and others again, having escaped severe injuries and lost their horses, were standing over their helpless comrades, and shooting down the scattered sepoys as they approached within revolver range of that gory spot. Indeed, in the tumult and hurry that prevailed, the black legs of these red-handed desperadoes were trampling over the bodies of our fallen as they rushed onwards to rejoin their main body, from which they had been cut off by the violent shock of the charge.

While all this was going on, the undaunted remnant—roused to almost superhuman efforts—having ridden into and over the mutineers, drew their revolvers, and an unrelenting and indiscriminate carnage ensued. And now the left squadron, noticing their comrades hard pressed, also raced into the *mêlée*; and then the clanking of steel, the rattling of musketry, the yells of the mutineers—which might possibly have been heard a mile off—supplemented by a wild chaos of sabres, bayonets, revolvers, and muskets, all mingled in a desperate hand-to-hand encounter. No quarter was sought, nor offered. In fact, these blood-stained ferocious demons had apparently determined to fight out their cause (?) or die in the attempt; and so fierce was their resistance that all the gunners to a man were killed and cut to pieces, fighting in defence of their gun, while the general slaughter was "whole-sale"; and it was only when a cannon-ball, like a friendly messenger from the approaching Brigade, suddenly hummed over our heads, that these *desperadoes* were startled into a retreat, and flinging themselves into the adjoining ravines, they soon disappeared in and among the deserted villages beyond.

This brilliant and bloody encounter marks, in the reddest of letters, a page in the annals of Volunteering. And I could transcribe from my memoranda a few notes on the heroic deeds that were done by many of my comrades during that desperate day; but those deeds need no comment here now, and are hallowed by my silence. This encounter also having terminated the struggle of the day, I once more for all quote from Brigadier Rowcroft's gazetted despatch (No. 241, dated April 19th, 1858), wherein the following paragraph is recorded, which speaks for itself:—

> I ordered Colonel Richardson, in command of the right squadron Bengal Yeomanry Cavalry, to move from my right flank, and charge this body of the enemy. The squadron, under its gallant leader, made a noble home charge; and though they came upon a larger body of the enemy behind a village, and the sepoys made desperate resistance, nothing stopped this brave cavalry, and they cut down and killed great numbers, and captured an eighteen-pounder gun with limber; and the enemy were completely dispersed.

Chapter 12

The Grave

I need not dwell upon the harrowing scene—the like of which God grant I may never witness again—in the hospital tent after the return of the Brigade to the camp; for the horrors of war and its attendant misery are bad enough to those before whom they are laid bare, without being revealed to those happily unacquainted with them. But so much of the scene may be noticed here, as relates to the native sympathy shown to us on this memorable occasion.

Our servants, and most of them were Mahommedans, wept and sobbed bitterly at beholding the distressing sight of human blood and suffering in the hospital tent; and as they diligently attended to the wounded, there was a marked sadness in the countenances of them all; whilst some of them, too, assisted in carrying to the graves the mortal remains of those who had fallen. So that, whatever may be thought of Mahommedan *tenets* as being fanatically prejudicial to Christians, here in the field, at all events, their genuine sympathy on our behalf showed that, after all, notwithstanding their fanatical instincts, Mahommedans, especially in humble grades, are always disposed to show kindness, and good fellowship towards all those who treat them with conciliatory forbearance.

After the action, the inhabitants of the neighbourhood evinced their joy at the complete discomfiture of the rebels by bringing in several wounded sepoys, who had crawled away un-perceived to some shelter close to Tilga, where they had received their final *coup de grace*. Of course they were summarily hanged on the nearest trees at hand, and with as little ceremony as one would use in slaying venomous reptiles. But, as I have long since thrown a veil over all such repulsive executions, I shall pass on, and not again allude to them.

In marked contrast, however, to these scenes too dreadful to forget, was witnessed on the same day a very impressive and af-fecting scene, when our poor fallen fellow-volunteers were bur-ied. Among them my chum, boon companion, and unchange-able friend in weal or woe, poor T——, killed while side by side in the taking of the gun. Yes, there the young, handsome, chivalrous fellow—a dandy in Calcutta—now lay in that for-lorn, out-of-the-way place, without as much as a blade of grass to mark the mournful spot. And as with heavy hearts we stood over those rough and shallow graves, and with moistened eyes gazed on the sad interments, our souls sickened at seeing the remains of our comrades, who but only a few hours before were full of life and chivalry, now being shovelled away into earthen holes like dogs. "Surely, God never created us for such a fate as this," was a remark more than once groaned aloud by the side of those premature and sorrowful graves. And although thirty-five long years have flown away on the wings of Time since those eventful days, and my hair is grey, in my mind's eye I have not finished gazing upon that mournful scene of sorrow.

It was satisfactory to find, by the arms and accoutrements of the enemy left on the field, that we had been punishing the fiends of several mutinous regiments; and as to the weapons of the Auxiliaries, no notice was taken of them, except that they were collected in loads and destroyed, together with the muskets of the sepoys.

Not once since the commencement of hostilities in this part of the country had the rebels received such a drubbing. They had been driven back on all sides, and routed without a prospect of being rallied; while their casualties in killed and wounded were enormous. Still, they kept up the "game of brag" by increasing their defiant salutes more than ever!

Campaigning affairs, like all human affairs, are in continual rotation; and this truism was here again verified by a swarm of rebels whirling round once more to a town named Tanda, and establishing chains of "military posts" there, as connecting links with the insurgents at Belwa.

With Oudh in a revolutionary blaze; Azimghur, the adjoining district, invaded by Kuer Singh's rebel army; and Gorukpur itself, offering comparatively a safe and central asylum, fast filling with marauding bands of insurgents, things began again to assume a threatening aspect. Reinforcements were urgently applied for, but none could be sent—not a man could be spared, while all European soldiers were required where they were. So that, in the very teeth of at least twenty thousand infuriated and exultant rebels, it was tolerably evident that the Brigade was expected to fight on, and hold on, where it was. And thus, it really seemed as if we had volunteered for a forlorn hope.

No doubt the Brigade would have continued to hold the position with the same indomitable resolution, and untiring energy as it had already repeatedly displayed in its defence, had not serious and unforeseen events now demanded its attention in another quarter. But I am anticipating, for the climax in the approaching hostile complications has not yet arrived.

By-and-bye rumours of night attacks began to pervade the camp, and in consequence the various guards were doubled during the dark hours, while the rest of the Brigade lay under arms, asleep with one eye open, until the sun was fully risen.

Bad tidings were also received from the rear, where a strongly fortified village, named Nugger, was threatened by a body of mutineers and their followers. Incendiaries, too, were active and busy; for hardly a night passed without some lurid conflagration lighting up the country, or villages blazing with such brilliancy that, had the rebels carried into effect their threats of hazarding nocturnal attacks on the camp, we should have welcomed them in the midst of these illuminations, which enabled us to see almost as clearly as by daylight. The land, in fact, was brimful of blood and fire; and had a stranger suddenly dropped down upon us from the skies, his first idea on the prevailing state of affairs would certainly have been that he had descended into the infernal regions.

Thus passed the turbulent interval between April 24th and 30th, with fire and thunder indicating signs of the coming storm. Clouds of horsemen, too, had been seen hovering about in the distance; while an incessant roar of heavy guns set in with the shadows of eventide, and continued with little intermission throughout that restless night, passed in harassing watchfulness.

It was obviously certain that the morrow, when it came in, would be accompanied with the warm work brewing; and now that the usual forerunner of the rebel tactics was once more astir, with nerves well strung we awaited another struggle.

And shortly after dawn, while the troops were hastily swallowing their breakfasts, the bugles, instead of the reveille, sounded the "assembly," and on our turning out instantly, we beheld the enemy coming down in three strong columns, with swarms of skirmishers moving in his front; and with such precipitation was his onset hurled at our position, that the Brigade was fighting at first actually to save its camp, into which round-shot ricocheted in rapid succession.

So formidable an attempt by a numerous and exult- ant enemy to overwhelm the Brigade, as it were, at the very outset of the action, thoroughly roused into headlong energy every man in our force; with the result that the camp was soon secure; and then the fighting from sunrise to sundown became general, and almost outlived that desperate day. To detail how the action was fought out to the end, how the missiles of war hailed around, how the sailors brought their guns to bear upon the crowded ranks of the rebels, how the infantry dauntlessly advanced, and the Yeomanry charged, would be to repeat an "oft-told tale," which in its reiteration could not fail to become wearisome, if not monotonous to a degree. I will therefore cut a long conflict short by stating that, on this occasion, we were successful in vanquishing the rebel army, only because we fought them in the united grasp of our concentrated force. Union was strength; and we presented a united front to the enemy. We were numerically too weak to cope with more than one column at a time; so that, throughout the whole of that terrific day, a desultory seesaw fight went on. When one column receded, another came on, and then another, and *vice versa*, until at length, as the sun sank beneath the western horizon, the enemy retreated, leaving a considerable number of his dead behind, and the Brigade the triumphant master of the field.

As a set-off to the victory, however, spies arrived in the camp almost at the same time as our triumphal entrance into it, with the astounding news that the station of Gorukpur was again threatened with invasion from the direction of Azimghur; that a skirmish with freebooters had taken place at a police post near the town of Buste; that the village of Cuptangung had been burnt to the ground; that Nugger having been occupied by insurgents, they were flocking into its fortress; and that the whole country lying between the ferry at Gyghat on the river Ghagra and the main road in the rear was blocked.

Then came the usual and oft-repeated question. What was best to be done? And after some discussion a sagacious decision prevailed.

It was urged that the present position of the Brigade was rendered useless by the enemy being in its rear, and pointed out that to hold it now would be to encourage him to break away, and overrun with impunity the neighbouring districts, which lay open without a bayonet to check his inroads and anarchy.

An immediate march, therefore, to the disturbed neighbourhood became unavoidable. And so, in a few hours after the above-recorded action, the camp was struck, the baggage packed, the earthwork levelled, and at midnight the terrific roar of the captured guns, as they were burst, appropriately served to convey a temporary farewell to Amorah, and an ominous growl to the foe in the rear.

CHAPTER 13

The Pursuit

Something like a guerrilla warfare having set in, with insurgents threatening our flanks, the baggage, etc., was directed to move between the tail of the Brigade and head of a strong body of all arms. But this precaution, however necessary, was the means of converting the march into a crawling, melancholy procession, resembling one following a funeral; and so tediously slow was our progress that the camp followers, in their impatience to outstrip an imaginary enemy, from whom no doubt they conjectured we were bolting, could not be restrained within the line allotted to them. Little therefore was our surprise when we heard that some grooms, who headed the Brigade by a few hundred yards, had been pounced upon by a band of marauders, and deprived of the valuable chargers they were leading.

It now became imperatively necessary to act, if possible, with greater vigour than heretofore, in order to summarily stamp out the seditious flame which had not yet ceased to burn, but, on the contrary, seemed rekindling again in this part of the country. Cuptangung, therefore, was no sooner reached than the Brigade, indifferent to the fatigue it had already under gone during the long night march, pushed on to the Nugger fortress, which being but a short distance off, we commenced to assault at daybreak.

Without much ado, our howitzers and rocket-battery were at once brought into position, and opened, as usual, with magnificent effect. Indeed, the splendid practice of the sailors with their guns on all occasions, was one of the admirable features in the scenes of our field operations, and nothing tended more to animate the fighting, than the grand spectacle exhibited in the unerring flight of their destructive missiles darting through space, like falcons descending on their prey.

While the guns fed death in the fortress, the infantry advanced against the outer fortifications, and soon became warmly engaged, but the resistance there, though obstinate, was quickly brushed aside; and then the bayonet cleared the place, excepting where the mutineers stood firm and perished; while those who fled, fell fighting to the death beneath the sabres and revolvers of the Yeomanry.

In the midst of the ruins and bodies with which the fortress was filled, loot of the most miscellaneous description was found. There were ponies, bullocks, cows, goats, sheep (all "taken in" probably for the sake of protection, though several had been killed and wounded). Then there were arms of all sorts, drums, pipes, cooking utensils, and what not? In using the interrogative, I abbreviate the long heterogeneous category of the spoil; but I must not omit to add to it the chargers which the rebels had but just captured from our grooms, and their recapture by us was considered far more important and satisfactory than the seizure and value of all the other booty put together.

An example in energy so effectual, and in execution so severe, gave confidence to the distracted peasantry, and exacted submission from certain turbulent villages in the neighbourhood.

The rebels at Belwa, too, who at our sudden departure from Amorah exulted in the belief that we had, metaphorically speaking, hoisted the white flag and taken to our heels, when they heard of the victory, were reported to be impressed with an idea that our retrograde movement, though ostensibly undertaken to reduce Nugger, was in reality a trick or stratagem, by which the Brigade hoped to draw them farther out into the open country, and thus lure them to their destruction.

Nugger having fallen, the Brigade was in a position either to remain where it now rested, or return to its former post at Amorah. But Cuptangung, offering as it did a wider range for field operations, and overlooking a greater expanse of the country, being rightly considered a more strategical locality, we halted there *sine die*; and again, by digging holes in the ground, we sought shelter in them from our "fiery foe"; and in the harassing routine of the camp duties, such as those to which I have already briefly alluded, the broiling month of May wore away.

During May the enemy received some vague rumours of an enormous force moving down from Oudh, and in consequence whole regiments of rebels, both horse and foot, were reported by spies to be hurrying northward with much alacrity and consternation. And by-and-bye these rumours proved so far correct, that a swarm of Gurkhas, returning to their homes in Nipal, passed by our encampment laden with the spoils of Luknow, and exultant in the "exploits" they had there achieved! And yet, forsooth, of what real assistance were these Gurkhas in their confederacy with us after all? No European who had an opportunity of seeing them before the enemy in the field could applaud their prowess; while the natives of Upper India regarded their interference in the war as a proof of weakness on our part, and, in consequence, the Government temporarily lost considerable prestige in those districts through which this superfluous Gurkha army sauntered homeward to Nipal.

While these Gurkhas were passing on, a lull in hostilities temporarily followed; but it was not allowed to continue for any length of time. For now Banse, a large and loyal town on the border of Oudh, was invaded by hordes of rebels; and as it was ascertained that they had resolved to advance farther into the district, the Brigade at once marched to Banse; while the perpetual and familiar booming of the enemy's guns marked irregularly the cadence in a long, fatiguing tramp, through a line of country overshadowed with the gloom of a night so black, that our eyes could not pierce its density beyond our horses' ears.

We crawled along—marching it could not be called—in a darkness that could almost be felt; and oft and anon, in the dead silence that prevailed in our ranks, an irritable mutter was all that could be heard. Now, without troubling to inquire what this "irritable mutter" suggested, there can be no doubt that some irritation in the Corps would seem natural enough, when it is remembered that for months and months we had been undergoing no ordinary torture from burning heat, and eking out an existence similar to that in which vermin, and reptiles are wont to thrive. And yet, although the neck of the rebellion had been dislocated by the fall of Luknow, our interminable troubles seemed still as dark as the night through which we were journeying.

To say that during this expedition we resembled half-starved brigands, is to suggest our appearance while living as best we could on the wing, like swallows, and on such food as astonished our stomachs. And as to our gallant and generous horses, poor brutes! they sobbed and hung their heads, and in their worn and wasted frames, they looked wretchedly gaunt, and as if on their "last legs" from the toil and torture of their daily life.

However, onwards to the "Devils" was the cry; so following our noses, and groping our way along the black and lonely road, we crawled slowly on and on, as savage and irritable as the present state of affairs had rendered us.

CHAPTER 14

The Sepoy

The descent upon Banse was effected—to use a vulgar phrase—by a dodge in our route, which, although edging on, as it were, towards that town, seemed to lead away from it, as well as from our actual destination. No doubt this "dodge" was meant to draw the rebels off the scent; but they were not fools, and proved themselves, in not being caught napping, quite as wide-awake as ourselves.

As we approached Banse dawn was breaking, heralded by the blush of the morning star visible on the horizon, and giving sufficient light to enable the outline of the town to be traced by our sleepy eyes; and as we scanned the place through the grey atmospheric film of early morn, no indications to show that the rebels had possession of it could be discerned anywhere. Presently, however, villagers appeared upon the scene, and enlightened us with news to the effect that the insurgents had abandoned the neighbourhood only but a few hours ago, and that Banse was quite deserted; and so on entering we found it. Not an inhabitant had tarried in the ill-fated town to witness its general wreck. All had fled, taking such goods and chattels as they could in the hurry of flight conveniently carry away with them, and leaving the remainder to the tender mercies of any one.

By this precipitate retreat of the rebels from Banse, it was consoling to anticipate another encounter with them in the open field, and also satisfactory to find the inhabitants restored to their homes, without their having suffered from our guns.

The population of this town was said to be well affected to the Government, and from the fact of their having been instrumental in saving some unfortunate European refugees from being massacred, it was but fair to acknowledge them as good and loyal subjects. Besides, on the present occasion, further proof in support of their genuine loyalty was shown by their returning to the town shortly after we had entered it, and supplying us with such refreshments as they themselves possessed, or could obtain from their neighbours.

One man particularly was indefatigable in his attentions to the members of our picket posted in the suburbs of the town; and so marked was his hospitality that we were naturally led to show him some civility in return. By-and-bye this man, finding that we were not quite so closely allied to his Satanic Majesty as the rebels thought us, became exceedingly communicative, and related many adventures that had befallen him; but nothing interested us so much as his story connected with a subject applicable to the events now under notice, and therefore I allow it to appear in these pages.

Sunker Teware (that was his name), though seemingly a man over sixty years of age, and with a frame enfeebled from inability to sustain manual labour, still retained that dignified demeanour characteristic of the high-caste Rajput soldier.

Sitting in the midst of us he said, in a voice broken by emotion—by genuine emotion:

"I was formerly a sepoy in the Bengal Army, but wounds and frost-bites having incapacitated me for military service since the Afghan War in 1840, I am a pensioner of that army. I deplore the deeds of blood by which India has been polluted."

And here finishing this prefatory flourish, he related to us so voluminous a narrative concerning the origin of the Mutiny, that I have not the space within the limits allotted to these brief chapters to more than summarily compress into a small compass a true translation of it; and I would ask the reader to bear in mind, as he peruses the story, that it is from the mouth of a *bonâ-fide* Sepoy, who, had he been in the ranks of the Bengal Army during the days of the Mutiny, himself would have become by his own showing a mutineer, like his brethren at that moment in arms against us.

The history of the Indian Mutiny in all its phases, and from every point of view, has been written until a host of uninformed people imagine the subject to be completely worn out, and well-nigh threadbare. But is it so? In reply I venture to say the subject is almost as inexhaustible today, as it was upwards of thirty years ago; and so it will continue, until every man who passed through that memorable epoch shall himself have passed away from the world. For there are thousands (Europeans and natives combined) still living who have a separate experience of their own to relate, and whose reminiscences would shed new light on yet untold incidents, or rather tragedies, of those eventful days. I need hardly add that I allude only to those men—like ourselves—upon whom the thunderbolt of the Mutiny fell, and not to those who subsequently aided in its suppression.

In fact, the stage on which that tragical catastrophe occurred was so vast in extent, and the actors on it so prodigious in numbers, that even at this distance of time numberless episodes of the Mutiny—all more or less laden with agonising sorrow—are unknown, and, alas! many never will be known; for hundreds of our unfortunate countrymen, who could have described harrowing and heart-rending scenes, perished; and their sad fate is understood only so far that to this day their unburied bones are strewn in remote jungles, or lie bleaching on many of the forlorn plains of Upper India.

And in corroboration of these cursory remarks, Sunker Teware's story would probably have passed into oblivion, had not we met him through the merest chance. As he told it, so I now proceed to tell it, although clothed in my own matter-of-fact words, as embodied in the following chapter.

CHAPTER 15

The Cause

Oudh—lying about the centre of the great sub- Himalaya valley, and watered by such magnificent rivers as the Ganges and Ghagra, as well as by many smaller though navigable streams was regarded by the Brahmanical tribes, from time immemorial, as the granary and garden of Hindustan.

The extraordinary fertility of its soil; its vast pastoral and agricultural resources; it's beautiful rural districts; its majestic forests; its handsome capital city (Luknow ranked next to the imperial city of Delhi); its splendid temples; its great traditions, like those appertaining to Bhinswara; its ancient memorials, like Ajudya, the birthplace of the far-famed Rama, whose name is the Hindu's Bond of Brotherhood over the whole of Hindustan; its grand martial race of men, like the Bhinswara Rajputs—all combined to make its proud and warlike people reverence the region as a " paradise," in which lay their homes, and the heritage of their offspring.

Notwithstanding, therefore, all that was urged to the contrary by interested "outsiders," the annexation of Oudh took its population by surprise; and from the hour in which this superb kingdom unjustifiably passed into the possession of the East India Company, it awoke from the slumber of ages, and became a mine of sedition, only requiring time to burst into flames of a sanguinary revolution, and from that day onwards its aroused Hindus and Mahommedans abided an opportunity to rise up against, and drive out the white interloper.

That this feeling rankled in the hearts of the people was manifested by the tumult caused in Oudh by a patriotic Mahommedan, named Fuzul Ali, who attempted to bring on an insurrection some six months before the Sepoy army rose in mutiny. And mark—yes, mark, reader—these very same sepoys were the men who hunted down this insurgent leader, and brought him to the gallows.

By the summary termination of Fuzul Ali's abortive attempt at revolution, the insurrectionary movement temporarily subsided—not, however, for want of sympathy with its cause, but because it was premature; the agitation being merely a convulsive start of the active volcano, which subsequently burst out so fiercely and blazed so high. This agitation, however, would unquestionably have vanished, as soon as the people became reconciled to the novel state of things under the new Government; but before the wounds caused by the seizure of their beloved country had healed, a new cartridge, from a concurrence of phenomenal circumstances, was "introduced" to the Bengal Sepoys; while, at the same time, this very cartridge actually became an irresistible weapon in the hands of the discontented and designing Mahommedans of Oudh, who at once discovered in it an instrument to aid them in striking a blow for regaining the kingdom, and they hoped to succeed in the attempt by working through its powerful influence on the caste superstitions of the native army.

From their compatriots, of course, they naturally anticipated unanimous support; for they were aware that the whole population was exasperated by the annexation, and smarting in common with themselves under a cruel injustice, perpetrated in the peremptory confiscation of their cherished ancestral lands-lands of their birth, and to their notions steeped in honey, and superior to all others in the world. Accordingly no time was lost in setting a gigantic conspiracy actively on foot.

In the infernal plot that was to create and ripen disloyal combination among the Sepoys, and produce the awful tragedies at which the civilised world stood aghast. Oudh, primarily, should be represented, figuratively speaking, as a charged mine, ready for explosion, and the greased cartridge, secondarily, as a lighted match in the hands of the Sepoy army—a match which, at the appointed time, was so effectually applied that, while it blew up the mine and shattered Oudh to atoms, it also convulsed the whole of Upper India, and shook the very foundations of the Empire itself.

Shortly, therefore, after the appearance of the greased cartridge upon the tragical stage, and not many months after the annexation, emissaries went out from Oudh into the North-West Provinces, and surreptitiously predicted that an appalling calamity was close at hand: that an unclean cartridge, greased with swine's and cow's fat, had been distributed among the sepoys with the object of converting them to Christianity; and that before long the whole population would be forced—if need be, at the point of the bayonet—to follow the example of their brethren-in-arms, as a matter of course!

What wonder, then, that this atrocious "prophecy," so to call it, had the effect of spreading alarm, like wildfire, throughout Upper India; and that consequently, in their credulity, thousands and tens of thousands of ignorant victims became thoroughly imbued with hatred to the Government! Indeed, within the memory of that phenomenal and venerable authority, the "oldest inhabitant," never were the natives of the North-West Provinces in so great a paroxysm of fear; and this fear, in an intensified form, ultimately extended to the Sepoys themselves, with the terrible results known to the civilised world. By way, too, of giving plausibility to the "prophecy," and for purposes as obvious as they were mischievous, unleavened cakes (*chupaties*), alleged to have been made by Christians, were sedulously circulated among the Hindu villages throughout Upper India. Naturally, therefore, this infamous treachery, preying as it did in a direct manner upon the caste bigotry or fanaticism of a superstitious people, also created a profound impression in their minds. Confidence in the Government was gone, while distrust and apprehension took its place instead. And the numerous tribes,

according to their several characters, were influenced by seditious excitement, or paralysed by their belief in the awful doom
with which they were threatened!

But even at this critical juncture of affairs nothing could have
severed the sepoys from their allegiance to the Government-
that is to say, in their own phraseology, they were "true to their
salt"; and with Hindus, this expression implies irrevocable and
unswerving fidelity to duty on behalf of those whom they may
be serving. And yet, when the Mutiny burst out like a sudden
conflagration, and startled India, one of the most popular be-
liefs about it, and one which has been fostered by many writers,
was that it had been brewing and in a state of fermentation for
years, and that it was an organised and pre-meditated rebellion;
whereas the revelation of the following facts opposes this falla-
cious theory, and renders it not only visionary, but stamps the
revolt in its suddenness as unpremeditated, and in its alleged
"organisation" as the strangest that ever took place. For when a
whole army—composed of sappers, artillery, cavalry, and infantry—divides, and subdivides itself, and flocks in thousands, some
to Delhi, some to Luknow, some to caste leaders or territorial
chiefs, and some again to their peaceful rural homes, where, it
may be asked, is the "organisation," or premeditation discernible in this veritable phenomenal movement, which actually occurred?

Besides, had the revolt been premeditated, or in a state of
incubation, so to speak, would it not have been hatched a year
or so earlier, when England was engaged in a stupendous struggle with Russia, and when in consequence India itself had been
denuded of European troops for service in the Crimea—to say
nothing of the war with Persia, which had just been brought to
a successful conclusion, and English regiments were returning
thence to India? Then, again, where were the good and faithful domestic servants, of whom hundreds were related by kin-
dred ties to the Sepoys themselves? Would not they have heard
some allusions to, or whispers of, the approaching evil days, and
sounded warnings of the coming disasters? disasters under which

they themselves reeled, and were struck dumb, while at the risk of their own lives saving those of many Europeans.

It must be borne in mind that I am recording Sunker Teware's sentiments in saying, that if ever an army mutinied without premeditation, that army belonged to Bengal; and how far the Mutiny was unpremeditated, I will endeavour to substantiate in another page further on.

Moreover, it must ever be remembered to the credit of these very same Sepoys that, only a few months before they rose in mutiny, they were actually hunting down to the death, or bringing to the scaffold so-called "rebels," or by whatever name one may designate men whose patriotism forced them to resist an unwarrantable confiscation of their homes in Oudh.

Perhaps, therefore, it will not surprise the reader to be told that Sunker Teware stated, as a solemn matter of fact, that the Sepoys, taking them all together, were never disloyal until, suddenly seized by a superstitious panic, and in consequence becoming literally mad, they rushed headlong, like a crowd of frenzied demons, into an ever-lamentable rebellion—into which he, too, would have been dragged, in spite of himself, by caste fanaticism, had he been, as he affirmed, serving with, instead of a pensioner of, the army.

While the plot thickened, and Upper India simmered with treason, and the echo of the panic, which had broken out among the Sepoys, re-echoed in all the military cantonments of the Bengal Presidency, the infernal conspiracy, in which they were to act the part of the principal tragedians, had accomplished its designs so successfully that by this time their distracted minds could think of nothing else—of nothing else but of their castes hovering, as it were, on the very brink of eternal perdition! And who can gainsay the fact that the high-caste Hindu of the Bengal Army of those days held his caste more sacred than anything on earth, and not only adored and idolised it, but would rather have died than lost it? Indeed, it is quite within the truth to say that it would have been difficult to point to any people, in the civilised world, more deeply imbued with reverence for their own souls, than were those Sepoys for their castes.

But this was not all; for while perturbed as they were at this momentous period by irritating doubt and fear, shoals of rustic letters, carefully detailing all particulars concerning the predictions that were in circulation, began to arrive among them from their rural homes. And these letters, while full of earnest exhortations, strikingly illustrated the danger to which they were exposed by the wicked and foul machinations of the authorities, and forcibly reminded them that if they were once defiled by the unclean cartridge, excommunication from caste and brotherhood, and banishment from home and family, would be their irredeemable lot for ever. Here, then, was the climax in the conspiracy; for the greased cartridge was actually in their hands, and the solemn warning from, their homes already too late.

Thus this incident, so sudden and appalling, drove them with horror and terror into a sort of bewildering panic. And panic is one of the most cruel of all manias; it is, moreover, infectious, and men under its influence are to all intents and purposes madmen. For instance, in the early days of the Mutiny even Englishmen exhibited aberration of mind to such an absurd extent that hundreds, actually in Calcutta itself, and at many other stations, "performed" a general and discreditable stampede to places of refuge, when there was really no cause for alarm. So, too, through the influence of a groundless panic, commenced a mutiny the like of which the world never saw, and by which an almost incomparably magnificent Empire—the Koh-i-nur of the world—the growth of more than a century, under the fostering care of some of England's most noble sons, was literally crumbling into dust and ruins in less than a day.

Here a member of our picket interrupted Sunker Teware by asking the reason for the symptoms of the Mutiny appearing first in those cantonments nearest to Calcutta, and thus, as it were, in the face of a vast European population, a strong force of English soldiers, an overwhelming number of sailors belonging to the shipping; and also while no sign of disloyalty had appeared among the sepoys in the military stations of the Upper

Provinces. His answer to this question was to the effect that, although the initial step in the direction of a mutinous movement was taken by the sepoys stationed adjacent to Calcutta, that initial step was accidental, insomuch that when the mutiny occurred there, every regiment in the Bengal Presidency was, more or less, already disloyal, and in consequence the initial outbreak might have happened at any cantonment. But, as already stated, there being no defined, or preconcerted organisation in the movement, all the regiments, fearing to initiate the "move," waited for each other to rise, and immediately the first successfully rose in open rebellion, the rest, "in Indian file," like imitative sheep, followed as a matter of course.

Meanwhile, alarmed at the threatening attitude now assumed by the misguided and deluded sepoys stationed at Barrackpur and Bahgulpur, near Calcutta, the Government strenuously endeavoured, with reassuring proclamations and conciliatory explanations, to quiet and soothe their aroused feelings. Just as if they were now likely to believe a word of the authorities! Nay, more; they would no more have believed even the solemn oath of the East India Court of Directors, than the population of Upper India would have believed, after the annexation of Oudh, in the honesty, and veracity, of any Englishman; from the highest, to the lowest in the land.

Consequently every effort to pacify and conciliate these mercenary, pampered pets not only failed, but encouraged them to insult the authorities; and therefore, under a vague impression, no doubt, that so severe an example would tend to crush the crisis in its infancy, two of the conspicuously disloyal regiments were summarily disbanded. But this fatal act, instead of realising the desired effect, convincingly proved as efficacious in its results as fuel does to a rising fire: that is to say, for a brief interval it smothered the lighted furnace; and under the temporarily subdued flame, things seemingly relapsed once again into their former peacefulness. Still, a feeling of bewilderment was abroad, and confidence had been too violently shaken to return as suddenly as the quiet days that seemed now to prevail; besides, it was felt that this delusive calm, was the ominous premonitory sign of the coming hurricane; and so in reality it proved, by overwhelming Upper India without apparent manifestations in its approach.

The mutinous sepoys of the disbanded regiments above alluded to, loosened from all restraint, and goaded with vindictive animosity, spread themselves over the length and breadth of the country, and on the way to their homes diligently proclaimed the immediate advent of evil times. Moreover, they took care, not only to exaggerate the state of things at the military stations from whence they had come, but to substantiate, as it were, the wild and seditious stories which were already implicitly believed by a vast community of the people.

All this while no Englishman in the Bengal Presidency would have believed that he, and his fellow-countrymen, were standing on a volcano about to engulf them within its flames. On the contrary, before the crack of doom was heard in Upper India, confidence and trust in the natives was felt to such an extent that all Europeans—men, women, and even children—travelled over the country without the slightest hesitation or fear; and wherever they went the people always greeted them most kindly, and with the greatest respect. Nor did the Government itself realise so grave a crisis as the near approach of a sanguinary and disastrous revolution; though it apparently seemed to hope that, in the extinction of the two mutinous regiments, the clouds which over- shadowed and darkened the Empire would soon pass away. And, doubtless, it was under the bane of this fatal infatuation, that a whole catalogue of melancholy blunders occurred at the commencement of the Mutiny.

Unfortunately that great, good man, Lord Canning, had but only just arrived in India, and succeeded to a legacy in the form of a rebellion, bequeathed to him by his predecessor in office, such as, in the history of mankind, no mortal man ever had to contend with. With his inexperience, therefore, he was in no way answerable for the amazing blunders that were com- mitted in the early days of the Mutiny. But "Officialdom" was responsible for those blunders, because "Officialdom" had passed the principal part of its life among the men with whom it had to deal, and with whom it ought to have known how to deal more especially with those Sepoys who happened to be in garrison stations with European troops. Their teeth should have been drawn, without any discrimination, on the very first symptom of disloyalty, in the very first regiment of the native army. Disbandment, as has been seen, did more harm than good. Disarming, although it would not have stopped the Mutiny, would doubtless have had the effect of postponing it, and so enabled the Government to gain time, and prepare for the coming storm.

But, what with vacillation, hesitation, red-tapeism, and the infatuated cry of the commanding officers against disarming their "loyal men," the contagious rumour of successful rebellion flew over Upper India with the rapidity of electricity, until the culminating point in the Mutiny having at length been reached, the consequences may easily be conceived. From that moment the darkened clouds of the impending storm began to close in and gather to a head, till they burst with all the fury of an irresistible tempest, and deluged the land with torrents of blood.

The above summary of facts is founded on Sunker Teware's statement, recorded in my journal on the day he made it; and, by what he has stated, it is transparently clear that, although the greased cartridge was so powerful a factor that it destroyed the loyalty of the Sepoys, the annexation of Oudh was, without a shadow of doubt, primarily, and solely, the cause that originated the Mutiny, and led to a tragical catastrophe without a parallel in the history of the world.

Turning to Sunker Teware, I asked him whether his statement would be corroborated by the mutineers themselves, and whether he was sure that the Mutiny resulted really from panic.

"I'll stake my life upon it, it did. I have been a sepoy long enough to know the thoughts and feelings of my brethren; besides," he added, with a broken voice once more, as if the recollection of the recent events was too much for him, "the minds of the sepoys had been wrought to such a pitch of furious excitement by treason giving vitality and expansion to the terrible belief of their bodies, and their souls, being on the very brink of defilement, and eternal destruction, that, maddened under contagious delirium of panic, they instantaneously plunged into a conspiracy of extermination; and, in the frenzy of despair, their very nature changed, and they became, what they never were before, cruel and inhuman in their determination to destroy those, whom they were convinced were about to destroy them."

CHAPTER 16

The "Company"

If the reader should be displeased with the above digression, and censure me for having, at this distance of time, raked up a wretched and cruel past, the best excuse I can offer is that the defunct East India Company has never been (to my knowledge) adequately exposed to public scorn for their iniquitous policy of territorial spoliation in the East. And when we come to reflect that the calamitous consequences which resulted from the Mutiny, were due to their tyrannical and rapacious acts, no words can possibly be too strong for their condemnation.

As an old Anglo-Indian I say, and I challenge contradiction, that, after the annexation of Oudh, the educated natives of Upper India despised and detested the very name of the so-called "Honourable" East India Company.

And why? Well, as the dethronement of the King of Oudh, and the seizure of his vast and superb possessions, was the last stroke of "annexation business" done by the Company before their extinction, and burial beneath the ruins of a policy they themselves had created for their doom, I will here venture to show (though it may sound egotistical; but why "egotistical," when—as all along—in my narrative I am only concerned to tell the truth?) why the natives despised the Company, and British rule became naturally odious and justly offensive, especially to the Mahommedans; on what grounds Oudh was annexed, and how the annexation was accomplished. And as I was on the spot, and had but too good an opportunity of being an eye-witness of all that occurred on the occasion, I confine myself—as invariably—to indisputable facts.

In the outset, it is necessary to repeat that Oudh was so magnificent a kingdom that any other in Europe would have been justly proud to have amalgamated it with its own. Consequently, the Company never ceased to envy and hunger for its possession; until at last, impatient at finding no justifiable excuse for pouncing down upon the prey (I use the word in no disparaging sense), they composed—needless to say, behind a screen, to shade it from the light of the outer world—a proclamation for its seizure. And the essential abstract of this precious document is as follows:

> Uniform extravagance and unparalleled profligacy, the grossest abuse of kingly power, and the most heartless disregard to justice (!) and that paternal care of his subjects which in every country forms the bond of union between the king and people.

As this much is the gist of the proclamation under which Oudh was annexed, and which, no doubt, was also intended to operate as charity is said to do in mortals, and cover a multitude of the king's sins, I need not quote further to warrant my asking: what would have been thought, said, or done had any attempt been made to confiscate, or rather usurp, a kingdom in Europe on so scandalously concocted a pretence, as the above-quoted abstract of the proclamation suggests?

Doubtless the king had his failings, as all men have. And admitting that Oudh was a broken-down kingdom, ruined by native misrule, did these reasons sufficiently justify the Company in summarily depriving him of his crown?

But in those benighted days—and I am speaking of far more than thirty years ago, mind—India was exclusively locked out from the civilised world, and regarded as a huge "preserve" for the families and friends—whose name was legion of the East India Company. It was a land in which you might have passed your whole life, and been in blissful ignorance almost all the while of the outer world. There was no such thing there as public opinion to checkmate wrongs; no railway or telegraph communication; no means of locomotion, excepting by the barbarous *palke*, which resembled a huge coffin slung on black poles and borne on men's shoulders, who, poor wretches, toiled and crept over the country with their living freight like beasts of burden—when, in fact, it took more than a month to accomplish a distance that now takes less than a day, and when a journey to Upper India from Calcutta or Bombay, required as much preparation and time as it does now to undertake a trip round the world;—no Independent Press to boast of. No wonder then, that the Governor-General of India in those days held the position—to speak plainly of—a despotic Emperor. He could say and unsay, or do and undo what he pleased, and when, and how, and where he pleased. And if any proof should be deemed necessary to confirm the accuracy of these remarks, all we have to do is to call up the recollection of Lord Dalhousie's great absorption—within five years—of territory, which in area was more than double the extent of Great Britain and Ireland.

Unpleasant though it is for me to go back to the recollection of those wholesale annexations, and to speak of them in plain language, they must be so spoken of; for there is nothing like plain language, asserted and pronounced in sweeping terms, when plain language is thus needed, and if ever it was needed it is in speaking of the scandalous annexation under notice. And I am speaking, I repeat, as an eye-witness of all that occurred on the occasion, and asking whether any civilised government ever perpetrated a more unwarrantable act of tyranny and injustice, than that hidden from the world in the criminal seizure of Oudh; and whether its proud, susceptible, and deeply aggrieved people, numbering at least ten millions, could patiently bear, and contemplate with indifference, such grossly wrongful deeds, and yet in the bitterness of their feelings refrain from the relentless and barbarous vengeance which, in retaliation, they subsequently inflicted when the opportunity came.

We now come to that fatal day of the annexation, when, only

about one year before the Mutiny, a scandalised army, armed with the disgraceful proclamation quoted above, crossed the Ganges into Oudh, to the exhilarating tune of bands playing "See the conquering hero comes!" Flags and banners fluttered in the breeze; generals looked exultant, ensigns big; the people groaned, the troops applauded; the guns saluted; and the trick was done. The coveted crown was torn off the regal owner's head, and placed on that of the usurping "John Company" the kingdom proclaimed part and parcel of his territories, without a shot being fired, or the loss of a single life; while the unfortunate king, overwhelmed with grief and tears, was trotted down to Calcutta, and lingered there in sorrowful exile, to all intents and purposes as a "State Prisoner." Think of that, reader, as a State Prisoner, poor fellow, until (in banishment for thirty years) he died.

Hence, without an atom of doubt, the Mutiny. And hence, alas! the sacrifice of innumerable innocent lives, whose precious blood will continue to stain the East India Company's historic records for all time.

It must not, however, be imagined that the king was powerless against this iniquitous usurpation of his kingdom. Far from that; for an estimation of the power at his disposal may be formed when it is explained that, although his trained army was comparatively small, it was backed literally by hundreds of thousands of armed high-caste auxiliaries, from among whom the Company's sepoys themselves were largely recruited; and who, in fact, mainly composed the Bengal Army. Moreover, he had the sinews of war— as it is the sinews of most things—money.

Besides, further proof of the armed force at the king's back can be adduced by mentioning the power and influence of Man Singh, one among many of the proud and powerful Hindu noblemen of Oudh, and a more dangerous man to the welfare of our interests in that province could not have been found in those days.

Now, notwithstanding the king being a Mahommedan—and Mahommedans and Hindus are very seldom amicably disposed to one another—on a mandate from him, Man Singh with tens of thousands of his armed Rajput tribe—born warriors, and although entirely abstaining from animal food, physically a splendid race of men, with handsome countenances, averaging about six feet high, amazingly strong, and withal remarkably athletic-would have risen as one man, and, with the aid of the king's trained troops, swept the invaders through rivers of blood out of the kingdom.

Another formidable chieftain, named Bune Madho (and I speak of both these men from personal experience), may be mentioned as possessing such influence over the Rajput population, as would have enabled him to double Man Singh's force, for the expulsion of the invaders.

But no. The king was, as most Mahommedans are, a bigoted fatalist; and as such it seemed as if he preferred losing a kingdom, with all the glory of his dynasty, and departing into exile and humiliation, rather than ignore the inexorable law of Fate, and disown his *tenets*.

Be that, however, as it may, and hard as the struggle must have been to him, he resigned himself to his "fate," and with meek dignity submitted to his bitter destiny. And the history of this dishonourable dethronement has not only passed into the traditional history of Hindustan, but also into that of the Mahommedan nations of Asia—where, we may rest assured, it will never be forgotten to be handed down hereafter, from generation to generation.

If I could peer into the dim and distant future, and venture to prophesy, I would venture to foretell that, in after ages, when glorious India, in her regeneration, and under happier auspices, has grown up to maturity, and risen to the zenith of her destiny in becoming one of the grandest empires on earth, her posterity, instructed by Hindu tradition, will learn that the annexation policy of the East India Company originated the Mutiny, and that that policy was also instrumental in leading the Usurpers of Kingdoms into the realms of oblivion forever.

Not a man in England would be better satisfied than I should to see the statements contained in this chapter refuted. But, alas! twenty-eight years' experience, together with having viewed the scene, and taken an active part on the stage myself, enable me to affirm that the plain facts stated are beyond refutation.

Sad as the contents of the above paragraphs are, I yet grieve to leave embalmed within this one—enfolded as if in a winding sheet—a black shadow symbolising, so to speak, a ghastly spectre, eternally hovering over the unhallowed tomb of the East India Company. And although inexpressibly lamentable as it is to dwell upon the harrowing reminiscences of one of the most cruel catastrophes on record, I make no apology for the digression, especially as it has enabled me to trace, however faintly, the darkest spot on the historic pages of British rule in India. Indeed, the digression might still be continued, but what is the good; except to add that the Mutiny, in one respect, was not altogether an unmitigated calamity?

For it resulted in the old order of things being rolled up like a scroll of stupendous failures; and from that eventful period a new era—the glorious Victorian era of righteousness—dawned upon benighted India, by kind Britannia generously lifting her up to a higher level of prosperity and happiness than that to which she had ever attained; and, as years roll on, she is destined to become, as I have already ventured to say, without any prophetic romance, a glory to Asia in her resources of civilisation; and in the far, far distant future, her lustre will tend to brighten the lot of countless millions of her people, and reflect the grandeur of the mighty English nation which, with its irresistible arm, benevolently dispelled the darkness in which she had slumbered for ages immemorial, and raised her to the dignity of an Empire perhaps second to none in the world.

And when communication by railway is established between England and India; and steam has annihilated the space across the Eastern and Western hemispheres; and the natives, in their regeneration, pass a portion of their lives amid the enlightening influences of European nations; and caste-superstitions have become humbugs of the past; and the representatives, or M.P.'s, of the Empire take their seats in the national assemblies,—generations yet unborn may see Imperial India, linked arm-in-arm to her foster parent—Old England taking her place among the foremost realms of the earth, as one of the most marvellous Empires that the world has ever known.

CHAPTER 17

The Rout

We now return again to the rebels.

Their position being menaced by "flying" columns scouring Oudh right and left, they deemed it advisable to " move on," rather than remain stationary, and thus run the risk of being intercepted by some of these columns. So leisurely, however, were their movements conducted that it would have been no difficult matter to have brought them within arm's length of the Brigade immediately after they had "broken cover," had not the Rapte, flowing between them and us, proved an effectual barrier. This river, in fact, so completely kept them out of harm's way, and arrested the object of the pursuit, that for days they must have laughed at our happy-go-lucky, and devil-may-care rambles over the burning plains, and in the blazing hot winds.

There can be little doubt that never in any war, since the world began, was the sun a greater enemy than in the Mutiny campaign. And some idea may be gained of the insufferable heat under his vertical beams, when I state the fact that we could not retain our feet in the burning stirrups, and the ground was heated to such a degree, as not to be borne by the naked foot. The dismounted portion of the Brigade therefore naturally suffered more in proportion to ourselves, and as they droopingly dragged themselves along the line of march, and struggled on with the hardships of their lot, they looked sun-dried, ghastly, and like ghosts, while a large number among them presented a pitiful appearance, with blood trickling down their sun-cracked cheeks and blistered noses.

But who among us cared to growl at exposure or hardship in those days, when we knew that all over Upper India tens of thousands of England's "war-dogs" were having their day like ourselves, and undergoing a similar process of roasting?

So, while dogging like bloodhounds the track of the rebels, they suddenly doubled round to Amorah once more, and made a stand there, on the same memorable battle-field, where they had already received so many fatal blows. And on our approaching the locality, we beheld literally an army of vultures settled down on the blood-stained plains on which we had fought so often, and so fat and unwieldy had they become on the flesh of rebels, that not one among their countless numbers seemed disposed to quit the scene of their festivities, or move out of our way as we positively rode through them, amidst shocking sights which, in compassion to the feelings of my readers, I pass over in silence.

On June 9th, when morning dawned after a night almost as hot as day, the dropping of long shots and the distant reports of muskets warned us to prepare for action; and the action throughout its main features resembled those I have already so briefly described.

In one respect, however, there was a novel exception, in our encountering the mutineers on this occasion before the sun had risen. They were accordingly punished with terrible severity. Drawn up in two divisions, and led by the usurper of the Gorukpur district, they fought with all the energy of despair, until the naval howitzers and Enfield rifles had stretched their best men *hors de combat* on all sides. Then the corps, *en masse*, were let loose in pursuit, and with hearts as hard as stones, and tempers rendered furious by aggravating exposure, they irresistibly swept over the retreating hordes, in the final scene of another sanguinary and crushing defeat.

The signs of the rainy season were now beginning to reveal themselves in the white, woolly-looking clouds, which in their airy flight had commenced to appear above the horizon; and these harbingers, so to say, of milder or cooler days were hailed with positive delight as, after the defeat of the enemy, we marched to Buste.

Here an agreeable surprise awaited us in the unexpected arrival of the 13th Light Infantry, under the command of the gallant Lord Mark Kerr. That many valuable lives might have been spared had this distinguished regiment joined the Brigade at the commencement of hostilities in this part of the country is self-evident, and so easily understood from the contents of the preceding chapters that it needs no comment in this place. But in passing, it may be noticed as some- what flattering to the B.Y.C. that, in welcoming the reinforcement, the Brigadier openly declared to the gallant new arrivals his belief that, but for the cavalry, his force would probably have been overwhelmed by the sheer numerical weight of the rebels. And the truth of this remark requires no confirmation, because the insurgents well knew that in action they were always within arm's length, so to say, of mounted men with drawn swords, who never did things by halves, and from whom they could not easily escape in flight. At the same time, too, they dreaded nothing more than the thundering clatter of our horses' hoofs at their heels, and our hard-hearted war whoop of "devil-take-the-hindmost" resounding in their ears.

The reader will remember that when we passed through Buste, half-dead from the effects of hardships, and privations sustained in the early part of the year, its inhabitants, instead of showing some sympathy in behalf of our deplorable condition, received us with scowls and growls; but the tide having now turned in our favour, a reciprocal change also came over the spirit of their insolence, and they at once became like brothers in their kindness to us all; so that Orientals, too, (though less civilised than Europeans in general) evidently understand the art of exemplifying the insincerity of this hypocritical world. When we were struggling with adversity, they stroked their black moustaches and scoffed at us; now in "prosperity"—if I may use the word to express our improved prospects—their professed friendship seemed apparently to have no bounds!

With regard to Buste itself, its suburbs had been transformed into a huge military cantonment, as by the wave of a magician's wand; and on our occupying the sheds and huts which had been constructed for the Brigade, we were indeed thankful for having at last got into even such rough quarters, as a harbour of refuge, after our merciless experiences and ruthless toil. But these pleasant reflections were soon dispelled by the indefatigable rebels having again reappeared in the neighbourhood of Cuptangung. Undoubtedly, their only object in displaying all this activity, was merely to harass the Brigade while the hot weather lasted, for they were well aware that the sun was as much our mortal enemy, as he was their powerful ally. But for all that, so soon as the shadows of evening fell upon the land, we were once more on the wing, with the prospect of attacking the "Devils" on the morrow.

As we crept along at a snail's pace in a sultry night, it was too dark to notice anything; but there was an ominous stillness in the air like that foreboding the approach of a tropical storm.

The hot winds had lulled themselves to rest with the sun, the country still panted with glowing heat, and the sky, though cloudless, was dimmed by a brassy film that obscured the stars. Suddenly from the far-off distance a dull rumbling sound resembling thunder was heard, followed by vivid flashes of lightning on the horizon. Presently we were unexpectedly kissed with cool puffs of wind, which instantly turned into strong gusts, and developed a howling hurricane. Soon flashes of lightning followed each other with amazing rapidity, and peals of thunder absolutely deafening, rolled onwards, louder, louder still as they approached, and yet louder than the roar of all our artillery fired off simultaneously. Then there seemed a momentary lull in the furious rush of the hurricane—as if to allow the forlorn creatures below to prepare for what was coming—while from the electrical discharge above descended a terrific crash, accompanied with oceans of rain seldom seen out of India, and which drenched us in a moment.

This perfect deluge assailed the Brigade about midnight, and brought it to a standstill; and although it poured down upon us in pitiless torrents until broad daylight, and every man was saturated to the skin and wet through and through, without a dry rag on his back for several mortal hours, we thoroughly enjoyed the refreshing "ducking," as a downright treat and relief to the fearful fiery torture we had helplessly endured so long.

Notwithstanding, however, this prolonged halt under a waterspout in the dark, and the road having become a river of mud, the whole Brigade reached Cuptangung before noon, and encamped under some of those well-known *pepul* trees which grow to such colossal size in India, and are "reverenced" by all Hindus, owing—as tradition tells them—to Old Buddha having invariably meditated and taught his profoundly beautiful precepts under the benevolent foliage of the pepul tree! Apart, however, from this hobgoblin of Buddhistic tradition, the *pepul* tree is a grand product of the vegetable kingdom, and its dense foliage will not only defy the rays of the sun, but its gigantic leafy canopy will effectually shade a whole regiment of a thousand men.

While on this expedition we realised, with raptures of delight, that the welcome rainy season had been ushered in by the recent thunderstorm, and which, in fact, was the herald of the periodical monsoon. And with its advent what a sudden transition from misery to joy; what a charming transformation in the aspect of the country, and the temperature of the atmosphere reciprocally occurred, to be sure! Only a few days before the whole face of the earth, as far as the eye could wander, was burnt up like a cinder; but now, within a week since the bountiful rain, all Nature, satiated with the refreshing deluge and washed clean, suddenly revived, and sprang, as it were, into new life, and came out in a new toilet. Over the refreshed landscape now stretched a rolling carpet of verdant grass; innumerable birds joyfully singing appeared upon the scene, as mysteriously as the thousands of frogs that found their way out from the bowels of the earth, and croaked in loud, unearthly chorus the return of cooler days; myriads of flying and crawling insects swarmed everywhere;

while we ourselves felt as if, at a single bound, we had unconsciously sprung from a perfect hell into an agreeable clime.

In other respects, too, luck seemed to be turning in our favour; for *Bazar* rumours—which in India are borne from mouth to mouth with almost inconceivable rapidity, and, though gathering impetus as they fly, generally are substantially correct—floated in the air, and predicted the approach of calmer times.

So that what with our being overshadowed by cool foliage, the delightful change in the temperature, and the remorseless burning winds subsiding, we could well afford to patiently wait for the absorption of the surface water round about the position taken up by the rebels, before striking them the fatal blow that shattered the last remaining hope—whatever that might have been—in the hopelessness of their "cause,"—a blow that struck them down to the ground, and from which they only rose again as armed fugitives in full cry, with their tails between their legs, like a pack of whelping curs flying before the wrath of superior dogs.

Moreover that stronghold at Belwa, having been evacuated by the enemy, was in the ravenous claws and paws of vultures and jackals. Hostile guns were now seldom heard; and incendiary fires for the best of reasons had long since ceased, there being nothing more left to burn. The villages lay in ruins and ashes; desolation and the gloom of death reigned supreme everywhere; and, wherever we went, the whole country looked as if a wave of fire—quenched with torrents of blood—had passed over it, and left nothing but human and animal skeletons strewn over its ghastly and disfigured face.

But from such desolate and hideous scenes, we passed into the darkness of yet another eventful night, and, under the guidance of some intelligent peasants, made a very hazardous detour, and got fairly in rear of the rebel position. Meanwhile our artillery and infantry, having waited for daylight, now advanced upon the enemy's front with such impetuosity that a general engagement at once ensued, and, amid the din of cannon and the roll of musketry, kindled a fire among our fellows that burst out in an appalling blaze along the whole line of the Brigade, without, however, silencing the rebel guns, which were sweeping with shot and shell the approaches to their camp. But, unchecked by this storm of iron, the attacking force bravely rushed on to carry the position. Thus far the conflict had progressed, when suddenly a body of mounted men dashing on to the plain occupied by us, beheld in their front, face to face, a bristling array of sabres flashing in the morning sun; and aware as they were of the irresistible line of bayonets approaching from the opposite direction, they turned round like men on wheels, and raced back helter-skelter to their camp, and spread an alarm there, probably to the effect that they were hemmed in on all sides. At all events, whatever alarm they raised, it resulted in a bloody and disastrous rout, followed by the loss of all their field equipage. From the effects of that loss they never recovered; and from that moment the peace of these districts was secured.

Thus the object of the expedition having been accomplished, we leisurely retraced our steps to Buste, where, without another hostile operation, terminated the first year's service of the Bengal Yeomanry Cavalry.

And on that memorable anniversary, which called up a thousand recollections, the corps assembled to hear the contents of a letter from the Government, addressed to the general commanding the Brigade. The mails from England, too, had been received in camp on the same day as the letter under reference, and there were, among those for us all, many letters from home for those whom we had buried in several forlorn and blood-stained fields, and where the rain and winds of the inclement monsoon, were now weeping and sighing over the lonely and premature graves, that were destined to be ruthlessly ploughed up year after year, during the agricultural seasons of tillage.

The following paragraphs are the only extracts from the Government letter, above mentioned, that need be inserted here.

During the last twelve months the Bengal Yeomanry Cavalry have eminently distinguished themselves, and the Government has repeatedly acknowledged their gallantry in the field, and their exemplary conduct on all occasions.

As there may be some of their number to whom it may be very inconvenient to continue with the corps for any further period, the Governor-General is willing to allow them to take their discharge at once.

The retirement of those members of the corps whose interests and prospects were at stake by their absence from their avocations having been sanctioned, forty-six volunteers—retaining many souvenirs of the campaign, in the shape of bullet-wounds and sword-scars; or shattered in health or constitution—amid the waving of helmets in the air on the points of bayonets and sabres, cries of "Bravo," and cheers from the whole Brigade, sheathed their sabres, and bade farewell to the corps forever.

CHAPTER 18

The End

The tale of the services of the Bengal Yeomanry Cavalry is told—and told unassumingly, in a mere nutshell, with the humdrum accuracy of history. And this tale adds another footnote to the annals of the Indian Mutiny. But, in conclusion, I have yet to add that during the rainy season the corps remained at Buste in profound peace. A market was opened in the town; the shops, as in former days, were filled with goods; and the commissariat having undergone resuscitation, improved its stores; sickness became less; the feeble began to get stronger, and by the time the monsoon had well-nigh run itself out, men looked in better health once more. After the rainy season, the corps was employed in some minor affairs with fugitive rebels on the Oudh frontier; thence it marched to Sultanpur, and was there "broken up"—not, however, without a splendid Notification in recognition of its services, gazetted and published early in 1859; and from which I transcribe verbatim only the following paragraphs:—

His Excellency the Viceroy and Governor-General of India in Council cannot allow the officers and men of the Bengal Yeomanry Cavalry to separate, without expressing in General Orders his acknowledgment of the excellent services they have rendered, and his admiration of their endurance, and of their gallant bearing on the many occasions in which they have come in contact with the enemy.

The Gazettes of the 23rd March, 27th April, 11th May, 6th and 13th July, 13th August, 12th and 19th October, 23rd November, 1858, and 11th and 18th January and 9th March, 1859, all testify that the Bengal Yeomanry Cavalry have borne a distinguished part in the several operations therein recounted.

Long marches, exposure, fatigue, and harassing patrol and picket duties have from the first fallen to the lot of this young corps, and they have borne the whole in a truly soldier-like spirit.

The Governor-General in Council desires to convey to the brave officers and men of the Bengal Yeomanry Cavalry *a regiment of which all who have belonged to it may be proud*[1] his best thanks for the good service they have rendered to the State, and in disbanding the corps, he wishes the members of it a hearty farewell.

The reader will have noticed that, in quoting the numerous Gazettes recounting the fourteen actions in which we were engaged during the campaign, I have mentioned only about half that number in the preceding chapters; and my reason for curtailing them, I ought to say, is simply because they so closely resembled one another in general feature that, had I described them all, it would have been almost tantamount to describing the same actions, as it were, over and over again.

And now, with almost the last drop of ink in my laboured pen, I have only to add that the above Notification was penned by the generous hand of that illustrious Viceroy of India, Earl Canning of immortal memory, who, in bidding farewell to the corps in such laudatory terms, has left no ordinary record of the men who voluntarily, at all personal risks, and at all personal sacrifices, rallied round him in the tremendous Imperial crisis through which India had commenced to pass; and who in those critical days of immeasurable anguish, when no Englishman in the Upper Provinces could call his life his own, stood by him in behalf

---

1. The italics are mine.

115

of the endangered Empire—not when succour had arrived from England, and British bayonets were gleaming over the country, but in the darkest hour of trial, when the gloom of despondency and despair hung like a pall over the Bengal Presidency, and the fiendish massacres of innumerable English families, had made Upper India like a vast Christian charnel-house.

Furthermore, the Viceroy, in thus generously recording the meritorious and splendid services rendered by this little band of devoted Volunteers, was doubtless influenced by the remembrance of the exceptional ordeals through which they had passed while aiding in the suppression of the Mutiny. For he well knew and could speak of their days of trial, of nights of anxiety, of hardships encountered, of dangers vanquished, of sufferings borne with heroic fortitude, such as none except those who had themselves experienced them could understand.

Above all—how far above, words silenced by sorrow cannot say—he was aware of the sad fact that a considerable number of the corps, in the flower of their youth or manhood, had lost their lives, while a larger number still shed their blood, in helping to crush a Mutiny that in unparalleled treachery, and tragical infamy, has indelibly tarnished, and forever blood-stained, one of the saddest pages in the saddest annals of the whole world; and over the ever-lamentable record of which, alas! the veil of oblivion can never be drawn. Finally, in memory of my departed comrades who died in the Bengal Yeomanry Cavalry, it remains to be said that, though their deeds of glory are not blazoned in letters of gold, the imperishable records of the memorable campaign, in which they lost their youthful lives, enshrine the sacred death-roll commemorative of their devoted services, and tend to immortalise the patriotic devotion by which that famous corps was animated, while passing through an ordeal as terrible as any that ever tested the daring audacity, and unyielding endurance of what may be called, a handful of dauntless and uncompromising volunteers.

Private Metcalfe at Lucknow

Henry Metcalfe

Contents

The Chronicle of Private Metcalfe

Enlisted for the 32nd Regiment of Foot on the 7th July 1848 at the age of thirteen years and two months; served at Chatham for eleven months. Embarked for India on the 14th June 1849. Landed at Calcutta on the 3rd November same year, after a stormy voyage, being in a very severe storm off the Cape of Good Hope on the 15th, 16th and 17th August, in which we were what sailors term, battened down between hatches without food or drink the whole of that time. We lost on that occasion two of our boats, the bulwarks stove in, our jib boom taken away, also our fore and main top masts, with their running and standing rigging. There was two and a half feet of water on the troop deck. Well, after landing we proceeded to a station called Chinsurah, about thirty miles from Calcutta. Caught the jungle fever at that place and was very near being carried off, but was spared for rougher work; Marched from Chinsurah to Allahabad on the 14th January 1850, a distance of 500 miles (not a bad introduction). Halted at Allahabad, and remained in the Fortress for the hot season, and which I thought very hot indeed. Marched from there on the following October for a station in the Punjab, called Jullundur, and arrived there on the 4th March 1851. That march was about 700 miles.

Remained in Jullundur until the following November, and marched for the North-West Frontier (where I saw the first shot fired in anger). Arrived at Peshawur on the 8th January 1852.

On the 10th March following, the regiment formed a part

of an expeditionary force under the command of Brigadier-General Sir Colin Campbell (afterwards the celebrated Lord Clyde). Engaged the enemy, which were composed of Afghan and Khybur (Khyber) tribes. After one or two actions and a few skirmishes in which we were successful, we marched back to quarters again, and in the following June were called out again to a place called the Swatte Valley, and the place was so situated in a valley between the hills, and so hot that I can scarcely describe it. It is hardly credible when I say that the heat registered 115 degrees in the shade. What must it be out of the shade? Indeed, I heard one old soldier say that there was only a very thin sheet of tissue paper between the heat and the heat of the Lower Regions. Be that as it may, it was very hot indeed.

However, between skirmishing and marching, counter-marching etc., and after two pitched battles in which we were victorious, we settled the enemy for a time, and marched back again to quarters.

Perhaps it will not be out of place here to relate a little incident in which the obstinacy and sagacity of the elephant was displayed. We were crossing the Cabul River (a very rapid river). We had two elephants drawing a heavy siege gun. When we came to the brink of the river the elephants would not budge a peg further, not even when urged forward by the native drivers' spears. When the commandant of the artillery found they would not move, he ordered up the master elephant to see what effect that would have on the refractory ones, but not a bit of notice would they take of him. Well, the master elephant had a tremendous thick chain attached to his trunk which he shook in the face of the stubborn ones, but not a move. At last, tired of remonstrating, he belaboured the two elephants with this chain till their roars could be heard miles off. The chain had had the desired effect. Without waiting for a repetition of the chain, they plunged through the river with their load, and we had no trouble with them.

We had hard times during our stay on the frontier (two years) and were very glad to leave it, which we did on the 14th January 1854. We expected to be ordered to the Crimea, but were reserved for tougher work in India.

Well, after a very long march we arrived at Kussowlee (Kasauli, near Simla) a station on the Himalaya Mountains, on the 4th March '54 (another very long march). Present at the great camp at Umballah (Ambala), under the command of General Cotton and General Fane.

Marched back to Kussowlee, and remained there in ease and comfort until the 9th of October 1856, when we were ordered to march for Lucknow, which was to be our future station, and which proved in the sequel to be a hot spot for us. However, we marched for it, and on the march cholera broke out, through which we lost 56 of the smartest and best men in the regiment. We also lost three women through cholera. I had a touch of it in marching through Umballah, but I suppose owing to youth and an abstemious constitution, I got over it.

We arrived at Cawnpore in December, and in marching into the station had the felicity of seeing that blood-thirsty scoundrel, the Nana, accompanying General Wheeler, whom he subsequently betrayed and cruelly butchered at the above station.

We left a depot at Cawnpore, consisting of three officers and their families, together with 87 non-commissioned officers and men, and also about 57 women and about 62 children, which were subsequently ruthlessly butchered by the orders of that fiend in human shape, the Nana. It is scarcely to be believed that he accompanied the regiment to church on the Sunday before we left Cawnpore for Lucknow, but it is a positive fact. I saw him myself riding in a beautiful phaeton, drawn by two splendid grey horses.

Well, we start from Cawnpore for Lucknow, which was to be the grave of many a fine man. We had our Christmas dinner (such as it was) at a place called Bonnie Bridge, the scene of one of brave Havelock's gallant deeds or feats of arms on his famous march to the relief of the beleaguered garrison. Well, after we breakfasted, my comrade and me took a stroll a little way from camp and came to a sort of hunting box of the old

King of Oude. We walked in and the place was decorated with pictures of native art. Amongst the rest was a rough sketch of the massacre of the British envoy and suite at Caball (Kabul) in 1840. While we were commenting on this picture in walks a very consequential sort of native. I believe he was in charge of the building. Be that as it may, he told us in very marked terms that as we were going to Lucknow, our stay there would be very short. We asked him what he meant, and he very soon enlightened us on the subject, *i.e.* that we would be thrashed out of it, as badly as we had thrashed the Sikhs out of Goodgerat (Gujerat), an engagement in which my regiment took part. I thought this was rather strong on his part and was about the first intimation of the great struggle in which we were subsequently engaged in. So I thought I would commence the campaign on my own account and perform on my native friend who was going to help thrash us out of Lucknow. Consequently, I let him have a straight one from the shoulder (natives don't like straight ones from the shoulder).

I repeated the dose several times, my comrade remaining neutral all the time. Well, we left Mr. Native not in a very enviable position, but there was very soon a hue and cry in the camp that several soldiers had nearly killed a poor native. The assemble was sounded, so as to enable this poor native to pick the culprit from the ranks. I may here add that my regiment was very strict as regards the ill treating of natives, so that I thought I had put my foot in it, so to speak. Well, when I saw all the preparations that were being made, I thought I might as well spare the regiment the trouble of parading, so I went to the orderly tent, saw the commanding officer and stated the matter to him as it happened. The commanding officer asked who was by at the time, and my comrade corroborated my statement. He then asked the native if it was me who struck him, and he answered in the affirmative, and the verdict was:—Serve you right. He was sent to the right about, and I was cautioned to be more careful in future, but we had plenty of fighting in a very short time, and thus I think I may fairly say I commenced the campaign.

We arrived at Lucknow on the 27th December 1856. After being in quarters a short time we were ordered to camp with three regiments of native infantry, one regiment of regular cavalry (native) one regiment of native irregular cavalry, one battery of European artillery, one battery of native artillery (horse) and a battery of guns drawn by bullocks. The whole of these native regiments subsequently mutinied on the 30th May '57. The object of this camp was for combined drill.

Well, after the camp was over and about to be broken up, the officers got up horse racing and athletic sports for the troops, European and native. The races and sports occupied three days, and during those three days that fiend Nana was at the races and sipping coffee etc. with our officers, and all the time was planning the mutiny. After the races we returned to cantonments, and on the following April heard of the mutiny at Barrackpore. We were then ordered to be on the alert. Well, in a few days the 7th Oude Irregular Infantry mutinied at our station, and my regiment had the office of disarming them. We dropped on them at midnight and had the assemble sounded for them. We formed three sides of a square, the artillery forming the head part of it. The guns were loaded with grape and canister. Of course, we were loaded with ball cartridge. When these fellows were ordered to pile arms they refused, but when the gunners were ordered to prepare and our lads to present, the gallant mutineers altered their tactics and quietly laid down their arms and scattered to their homes, but afterwards they appealed to Sir H. Lawrence to be enrolled again. He, good-natured like, believed them when they promised to be faithful, but after the remainder broke out they did the same and were about the greatest scoundrels we had to deal with, for they knew all the holes and corners of Lucknow.

Next came the massacre of Meerut, and then we were ordered to watch the sepoy cantonments, which was very rough and hot work, both day and night at it. The next thing we heard was the mutiny and massacre at Delhi. In fact, almost the whole of the sepoys in Bengal were in a state of mutiny about this time, and the little garrison at Cawnpore under General Wheeler was surrounded by the Nana's horde of savages. It was hard to hear that our countrymen, women and children, were only 48 miles from us and we could not go to relieve them, nor could they come to us. Alas, we never saw them more.

Well, on the night of the 30th May these regiments mutinied. There were the 13th, 48th, and 71st Infantry, 2nd Cavalry, and half the native battery artillery. They broke out just as the gun fired for tattoo. They rushed with the yell of demons, but we were prepared for them. Their rush was intended for the officers' mess tent, but they met with a nice reception. Our guns opened on them with grape, and half my regiment fired a volley at them, which made them scamper, back again, to their own lines. General Anscombe asked our colonel to let him have half the light company of my regiment so that he, the general, might go into the sepoy lines and pacify these wretches, but the colonel tried to dissuade him from going near them in their then excited state, but he was not to be dissuaded from his object.

The general thought that if he only showed himself among them it was sufficient to quieten them, as he formerly commanded one of the regiments, and thought his men would do anything he told them. But he reckoned without his host. No sooner than he showed himself than they rushed at him. He then saw his mistake and thought to rectify it, but he was too late. As soon as he turned about to return they fired at him and killed him, so that a general officer was the first I saw killed in the great mutiny.

These mutineers began pillaging the officers quarters and then setting them on fire, so that in less than an hour the whole of the sepoy cantonments were in a blaze, and woe betide the hapless European who fell into their hands. There was a Captain Grant who belonged to one of the revolted regiments, I forget which. This man was on guard and his men turned on him and butchered him, but before he was killed I heard that he gave a good account of four of the rascals. The next was a young cornet of the 2nd Light Cavalry. This young lad was lying in his quarters when they rushed in and put an end to him, poor lad. He could not be more than 16 years old. The next was a young lad of my regiment, who was returning from paying his foster-father a visit at a place called Seatapore (Sitapur), about thirty miles from Lucknow. His time was up on the night of the mutiny and he was making for the cantonments when he was met by these scoundrels and butchered most frightfully, so much so that his nearest friend could not tell a single feature. The only way that we could tell was by his inside garments being marked with his name and regiment number. Well, that night, 30th May, we organised a small force and thrashed these fellows out of the station, and we recaptured two of the field guns that they took with them.

We did not follow them very far as we were rather jaded. We returned and remained under arms the remainder of the night. The next morning a portion of the three sepoy infantry regiments came into cantonments with the colours and arms. They surrendered themselves and told the commanding officer that the remainder were drawn up in battle order on the race course waiting for us. Well, we did not like to disappoint these gallant black sons of Mars, so we went for them, and sure enough, there they were waiting for us formed into line with their guns in the centre and flanks and their skirmishers thrown forward, but we very soon made them change their position for a fresh one. As soon as we opened fire and made a few gaps in their ranks they took to their scrapers and bolted off to Seatapore, not however, before we took two of their guns and thirty prisoners. The latter were subsequently hanged.

I mentioned a lad who was butchered by these mutineers when returning from his foster-father. Well, when the Seatapore sepoys heard of the mutiny at Lucknow, they also followed suit and this young lad's foster father was sergeant major in one of the regiments. His wife and children were with him at the time and these fiends rushed in and attacked them. The sergeant major, when he saw that they were making for his wife and little ones, (the wife was enceinte at the time), he laid about him with a vengeance. He killed six of these brutes before he was himself overpowered, and that was not before his only weapon of defence, which was his regulation sword, broke in two. However, he saved his wife and children, for while he was engaged with his opponents his wife and children managed to make their escape to the jungle, not however, before she received a bayonet thrust in the abdomen, which terminated fatally in the residency of Lucknow, where she and her little ones arrived after being wandering about the jungle for ten days, and when the poor woman heard of her husband being killed she could not be comforted and would not allow anyone to dress her wound. Consequently gangrene set in, and put an end to the poor creature's suffering. She was one of a great many who suffered at the time.

Well, after this we were on watch day and night after these fellows were beat out of Lucknow, for they promised to pay us a visit again at Lucknow, and indeed most faithfully they kept their promise. In the meantime cholera and smallpox broke out amongst us, so that we were in a pretty fix—and our friends (save the mark) were steadily approaching Lucknow for the sole purpose of putting us all to the sword. Consequently Sir Henry Lawrence (Peace be to his soul, for I believe a better man nor Christian was hard to be found) ordered us to retire on the Residency of Lucknow and a small fortress called Muchee Bhaun. These two places were put in a state of defence by erecting batteries etc. and our forces were divided between the two positions, which commanded the two bridges over the river Ghoomty.

It was my luck to be stationed at the Muchee Bhaun Fort. Well, when we arrived at our different posts on the 29th June, Sir H. Lawrence held a Council of War. He told his subordinates that he had received news to the effect that a force of mutineers were approaching Lucknow and were near to a place called Chinut, on the Fysabad road. Well, the conclusion come to was that we should march out and give them battle, (fatal error as the sequel will show). This force of rebels were composed of the mutineers of the whole kingdom of Oude. We were given to understand that there were only 5,000 of the enemy, but we found out our mistake when we got (nearer). However, we marched out to meet them with all the available force at our command (for we had to leave a portion of our force behind at both places to hold them and protect the women and children from the mutineers in the city, so that our force was comparatively small to them). However, our hopes were strong and we thought we could thrash all before us, but we were sadly taken in. Our force consisted of the following:—about 360 men of my regiment (32nd) and the battery of European artillery. Two heavy guns drawn by elephants (which were upset into a ditch by the native drivers and consequently had to be left behind for these scoundrels of native drivers cut the traces and drove the elephants off to the enemy). We had also half battery of native artillery, and a few Sikh cavalry. A few gentlemen and volunteer cavalry, and about 300 sepoys who remained faithful to their salt. This composed the whole of our force to meet, as we thought, about between 4,000 and 5,000 of the enemy, which as I said before we could easily dispose of, and I firmly believe we could if treachery had not been at work. However, when we got to Chinut we found out that the 5,000 was only a myth, comparatively speaking.

When we formed up and commenced the action we had not much time to consider our position, for we were very soon surrounded and the 5,000 turned out to be nearer 10,000. Well, the native artillery got the word action front, that was to commence the action. They instead galloped to the front and commenced the action by firing the contents of the four guns into us (this was commencing the action with a vengeance). They then limbered up and galloped to the enemy, which received them with yells of joy. I believe this was a preconceived plan with our foes. Well, with our two heavy guns rendered useless, and the others deserting, we were left in a nice fix, and in less than three quarters of an hour we had nine officers and 117 sergeants and rank and file and two buglers *hors de combat*. But why prolong this dreadful mistake. (I can call it nothing else.) Suffice it, we had the order to retire on Lucknow the best way and in the best order we could, and we did retire, not however, before every round of ammunition for the field battery was fired away. The first man that was killed was Colonel Case, as nice an officer and as good as ever drew a sword. He belonged to my regiment and was only after coming back from England where he had been to get married, so that his wife very soon became a widow, as so did a good many more before the struggle was over.

Talk about the present wars, why they are only child's play compared to that. Well, I may add that only for the gallantry displayed by the few cavalry (for indeed they performed prodigies of valour) we had (been destroyed). Indeed, there was one man by the name of Johnson who was a transfer from the 9th Lancers to ours. This man was one of the volunteer cavalry. He saw that one of our guns was in danger of falling into the hands of the enemy as all the drivers were killed. He immediately jumped off his horse and jumped on the battery horse which was leading and in the face of the enemy galloped off with the gun to Lucknow, and this prevented the gun from falling into the hands of the enemy.

This man was recommended for the Victoria Cross, which he richly deserved, had he lived, but fate ordained it otherwise for the poor fellow died during the subsequent siege of cholera. But as I said, only for the bravery of the few cavalry and the cowardice of the enemy, not a man would have reached Lucknow, for when taking into consideration the tremendous odds against us, together with the excessive heat of the weather, for it was on the 30th June, it may be easily imagined our condition and the fact of the poor fellows not having broke their fast, that everything was against us.

I saw on that retreat some of our finest soldiers drop down with sunstroke, never to rise again. I saw one fine young fellow who was wounded in the leg. He coolly sat down on the road, faced the enemy, and all we could do or say to him would not urge him to try and come with us. He said—"No, you fellows push on, leave me here to blaze away at these fellows. I shan't last long and I would never be able to reach Lucknow."

He remained, and was very soon disposed of, poor fellow. Another instance of brotherly love and self sacrifice. A bonny young man, by name, Jones, was being conveyed back on a gun carriage after being wounded. Saw his brother being struck down with a bullet from the enemy, and without the least warning he jumped off the limber on which he was riding and joined his brother to be killed with him. Another man, maddened by the heat and fatigue, charged in single-handed into the ranks of the enemy and was soon put to rest. Several other instances which I witnessed on that disastrous rout (which I can call it nothing else) I have not space for here, and I fear would only prolong a series of disasters which might have been avoided, but *Homme prepose—Dieu dispose.*

Well, after great trials we reached the iron-bridge, which luckily for us was in possession of some of our men under the command of an officer from the Residency (Lieutenant Edmondstone [1]) which were left behind when the expedition started.

They defended the bridge most gallantly, and covered our further retreat to the Residency and Muchee Bhaun. The latter place was where I was stationed, and on our arrival I saw several men drop down with apoplexy and fatigue. Indeed, I am afraid if the enemy were not checked at the Iron Bridge, we would be able to show them a very feeble resistance indeed. As it was, we were not called upon to do so that day. Whether through the resistance they met with at the bridge or the fact of their being satisfied with their victory at Chinut I cannot say, but suffice it, they did not attack us that day and when Sir H. Lawrence and the heads of departments compared notes, they came to the conclusion the fort of Muchee Bhaun, where I was stationed, had to be abandoned, and retire on the Residency, which we did on the night of the 1st July and blew the fort up. I happened to be with the last party who left the fort, as a portion of my company acted as a covering party to cover the retreat of the others, and so well was the whole affair arranged that the enemy kept

---

1. See *Notes* Lieut. Edmondstone's Letter

pounding away at the old place till long enough after the place was vacated and we safely landed at the Residency, and when the magazine, which contained all the powder, shot and shell etc. was blown up by our men, the enemy thought they had done it by their incessant firing of shot and shell, and they gave such a yell of triumph that you would have thought, with Shakespeare, that Hell had become uninhabited and that all the demons were transferred to Lucknow. After we got into the Residency, I shall never forget the heart-rending scenes. Mothers and relatives, who clung as a last hope that their lost ones might be with the survivors of the Muchee Bhaun party, but poor things, in most cases they were doomed to disappointment. Mothers asking for sons, wives for their husbands, it was heartbreaking, and rest or sleep was out of the question for that night and indeed for many a subsequent night. [2]

And now I may safely say the great siege of Lucknow commenced and history I suppose has faithfully chronicled how it was carried on and how it was ended, with its vicissitudes etc., but a few incidents pertaining thereto and which came under my own observation I hope may not be out of place.

Well, on the morning of the 2nd July my company were posted at a place called Dr. Fayrah's Bugalere (Dr. Fayrer's Bungalow where Sir Henry Lawrence died), and that post was to be the headquarters of the company while the siege lasted, but occasionally we sent parties to form outposts to more exposed places, and indeed, these posts in too many cases proved forlorn hopes to many a fine young fellow. However, we had to take our chances and trust to God and our weapons, which we had a good supply of the latter. On the morning of the 2nd July our position was attacked from all quarters and indeed very determinedly, but we repelled all their efforts on that day, and you may depend we were very glad when they took it into their head to retire within their position for that day at all events.

And now about Sir H. Lawrence. On that day, while sitting with his staff in his room in the Residency, a shell was fired

2. *Idem*

into his room but without doing any damage, except the hole it made in the wall. His staff urged him to leave his present quarters for fear of any harm occurring to him, but he treated the circumstance very lightly, saying, they will never fire another shell into the same place, but on the next day a shell came into the exact place and exploded, and a splinter of said shell hit Sir Henry in the groin and terminated his earthly career, which was not only a noble but a Christian-like and useful one, and the country lost not only a brave but a valuable servant, and the Garrison lost its right arm, indeed, only for the foresight of Sir Henry, I am almost sure we would never be able to hold our position as long as we did, for by his judgement and tact he could see what was coming, and he set about provisioning the place from all sources, and well it was that he did so, and his loss cast a gloom on the whole garrison. He, when he found his end was near, sent for Colonel Englis (Inglis) of my regiment and Major Banks— handed over the entire command to Colonel Englis and the Commissionership (which he held himself) to Major Banks. The latter was killed during the siege and the former survived the siege and was promoted to major-general and K.C.B. all in the space of five months. Quick promotion you will say, but it was nothing extraordinary in those days. Well, the last words he uttered were—"Dear Inglis, ask the poor fellows who I exposed at Chinut to forgive me. Bid them remember Cawnpore and never surrender. God Bless you all." And thus ended the life of a gallant soldier and a true Christian. He is in Heaven.

By this time and by some means the authorities heard of the dreadful massacre of Cawnpore and all the garrison of Lucknow proved how well they kept their promise never, with their lives, let the women and children in their charge fall into the hands of the enemy. How they kept that promise the world knows.

And now to mention a few incidents which occurred during the siege. One morning in the early part of the siege, I was sitting in the veranda of the house where we were stationed. A gentleman came out of the house and held a beautiful white terrier dog by a chain. He asked one of our men if he would shoot the dog as he had not the wherewithal to feed the dog as he was only a lodger in the doctor's house, and he had not time to bring anything with him into the Residency and had to live on the bounty of strangers. Well, this man (I mean the soldier) said he would shoot the dog as he wanted to empty his piece for the purpose of cleaning it, and he would have done it had I not interposed and asked the gentleman if he would let me have the dog to keep, and he said I would not be able to keep him as my allowance was too little for myself. I replied it did not matter, I would share my little allowance with the dog if he would let me have it. He consented, and the dog's life was spared, and a valuable one it proved to me, which I will explain as I go along.

The gentleman who owned the dog proved to be the Church of England Chaplain, the Rev. P. Harris, whose good works during the siege was highly spoken of and mentioned in Sir John Englis despatch of the siege of Lucknow. Well, I kept the dog and shared with him my scanty allowance of food which he, the poor dog, seemed to appreciate. Well, after a few days the gentleman called me to him and told me the history of the dog. He said that when he was stationed on the frontier, himself and his good lady were in the habit of attending the sick soldiers and were very kind to them, and one man in particular of the 75th Regiment. Well, this man did not know how to properly show his appreciation of their kindness, but asked the lady if she would accept of a little white terrier puppy and be kind to it. She took the puppy and promised the dying soldier that she would not part with it except through sheer necessity. The soldier died and the lady kept the dog to that day, and that was the dog that I became possessed of. "And now," said Mr Harris, "if you and Mrs Harris and myself survive the siege, will you promise to give the dog to Mrs Harris again?" and I promised that I would, and I kept my promise. [3]

And now to show what soldiers generally think of worldly matters in war time, and your humble servant in particular, Mr

3. See *Notes* Extract from Mrs Harris's Diary

Harris on this occasion said he would never forget me, and I believe he has not, and said anything that he could do for me he would, and I am certain he would keep his word too if I troubled him. He asked me then if there was anything he could do for me. I considered for a while and came to the conclusion that I wanted a pipe, as the only one I had was taken from me by somebody who thought he had a better right to it than me. Consequently I considered he would be conferring a great favour on me by getting me one. Accordingly I asked him for a pipe. He stared at me, and everything considered, well he might, for when he was considering how he could forward my worldly prospects, I only thought of the worldly pipe.

"Well," he said, "Metcalfe, you have almost stunned me, for I was thinking of something else, but I must see if I can get you one. I don't smoke myself or I might have no difficulty in getting you one."

However, he went into the house and told his tale about me and the pipe, which caused a general laugh. He could not obtain the pipe however, but instead he presented me with a box of beautiful cigars. After this, the dog accompanied me wherever I went, both day and night, and indeed, it was a good job on some occasions, for when on sentry at night and when the least sign of drowsiness came over me, the dog was sure to notice it and catch my trousers between his teeth and shake me to keep me awake, for it was very hard indeed to keep from getting drowsy considering being belted and under arms day and night, and never had our boots from off our feet for five months. But more about the dog anon.

The siege continued without intermission. Constant firing and alarms both day and night, till the 20th July when we had an intimation that the enemy were about to attack us from all quarters, and the brigadier went round all the posts to see that everyone was on the alert. The officer commanding my company was having his breakfast at the officers' mess and I was ordered to go and apprise him of the brigadier going round. I did so and as I was coming back who should I meet but the brigadier and staff. Of course, he must ask me what I meant by being absent from my post when there was an attack expected. I told him the reason, which turned his wrath from me to my captain, and as the brigadier passed me I thought I would wait and see the up-shot of the meeting between him and the captain, so I stepped behind a clump of bamboos and had not long to wait, for on the captain coming from the mess, the brigadier met him and the language between the two was very hot indeed. However, about 10.0 o'clock the game commenced, and a stiff game it was.

The enemy opened the ball, by blowing a mine which was laid for the Redan Battery, so called after the great Redan in Sebastopol, but of course, nothing to be compared to the latter. However, they miscalculated the distance and a good job for us, for their intention, to use a nautical phrase, was to board us in the smoke. Well, on they came like so many demons in human forms—all round the position with their bands playing all our national airs, their bugles sounding, flags flying, etc. Scores of times they advanced to the charge and of course, on each occasion were beat back. They kept this game up all day till we were nearly fagged out, and indeed we thought they would force us, but God ordained it otherwise. About 5 p.m. they gave up the job. [4] Now the position of the Residency was almost divided by a road from the Baily Gate, and on this road we placed a battery of four light field pieces, so that if the gate was forced we could play on the party who would force it.

If this gate was blown down or burnt, the communication between the positions would be partly cut off, for they had a bat-tery immediately in front of this gate, and the fire from it would completely sweep the road that divided the position. However, this did not occur, but they tried to burn the gate, and indeed almost succeeded, for the gate took fire and there was volunteers asked for to extinguish the fire. I was one who volunteered for this job, which was rather tough whilst it lasted. They kept up such smart fire of musketry while we were engaged in putting

4. See *Notes* Lieut. Edmondstone's Letter

out the fire. We succeeded with only two men slightly wounded. Well, after this to prevent a repetition of the fire we had another loophole cut in the side of the wall so that we could see if there was anyone approaching from an opposite direction.

Well, on the 10th August about 5.0 p.m. I was sitting on the veranda conversing with a young lady, the name of Alford, whose father was colonel of one of the regiments which mutinied. She told me she was only just after coming out from England after finishing her education, when the mutiny broke out. Rather a fiery reception for her, you would say, but such was the case. However, she said to me she believed the enemy would force their way in in the long run. Yes, she went as far as to say that they would attack us that night. The Baily Gate would be the place to be attacked. Whether she had a presentiment or not I don't know. I told her that if they made the attempt it must be done while I was on sentry at the new post, for after my time the moon would be risen and the attempt would not be made.

Well, I went on sentry accompanied by my dog. I sat down on an empty case with my firelock between my knees, thinking over the conversation of the afternoon. Just now the dog gave me the usual signal by biting my trousers. I looked through the loophole and sure enough, there was two of my sable friends. One had a bundle of tarred wood on his head, the other was after planting a bundle against the gate. I got my piece through the loophole and took deliberate aim at one of my friends. I could not fire at the two at once. They were not in a position. However, I knocked one over, and the other did not remain to be accommodated with a like dose. However, the gate was saved and remained so till the relief, and I may say that the dog was partly instrumental in saving it.

Next day there was a very severe attack, which lasted a considerable time. In one or two places they effected breaches and were just on the point of storming the breaches when they were routed by hand grenades. Some got under the walls and placed the ladders against the walls with the object of scaling, but their hearts failed them. Then they were afraid to run back for fear of being killed on the road, thus remaining to be treated with hand grenades, which medicine did not agree very well with them. We beat them off on that occasion, and had a short respite for a few days. During this time Havelock was making rapid strides towards our relief, but owing to sickness and paucity of numbers was forced to retire and await further reinforcements. "Hope deferred maketh the heart sick" was truly applicable to us. However, on we kept, hammer and tongs, day and night. One time chilled with heavy rain, another scorched with the sun. In the meantime, sickness and bullets were making sad inroads in our numbers, and things began to take on a very gloomy aspect, especially when we found out that Havelock was obliged to retire. They were continually mining and our people counter-mining, and indeed, our people and the enemy miners on more than one occasion met and had hand to hand conflicts, in which our people were victorious, and destroyed their mines. [5.]

I am now about to mention a few miraculous escapes. This is one instance. One evening a comrade of mine came to see me, and asked me if I could obtain a tot of rum. Well, I did not care for my rum on that occasion, and I knew if I wanted it I could get it from my friend Mr Harris, so I let him have my tot of rum. He put it in a small bottle, and said this will do nicely, for when I am going on sentry. He left me in a little while for it was a hazard to be absent from your post for any length of time. Well, about 10 o'clock at night I was on sentry on a heavy siege gun. It was a beautiful night, as calm as possible, and very little firing for a wonder. Just now I saw a shell being thrown from the enemy's position and going in the direction of the tot of rum. I remarked at the time that the shell was going in the direction of Jem, meaning the rum chap—and sure enough it did.

It landed at the exact spot, exploded and pitched the rum chap into the trench, smashed the little bottle which contained it, and which was under his head, for he was lying down at the time, also tore the pillow which was under his head into frag-ments; wounded Major Low and one or two others, and strange

5. See *Notes* Colonel Inglis's Letter

to say, never hurt the individual who it pitched into the trench, except stunning him for the time being, and when he came to himself his first enquiry was "Is my dram of grog all right?"

And one of the officers who heard this, laughed, and said, "I'm afraid not, my man, but never mind, I will give you one since that's all you care about."

You will wonder perhaps about me seeing the flight of a shell, but it was quite easy for a spherical shell fired from a mortar does not attain the same velocity as the elongated shell of the present day, and besides, the fuse which is attached to the shell to explode on its arrival at its destination emits sparks all the way in its flight, so that you may easily trace its direction. I felt rather uneasy on account of my friend's safety, so I paid him a visit the following morning when the above tale was told to me, he remarking at the time that he would never be killed after that. It would just as well if he had been for the poor fellow was reserved for a more painful and lingering death. That night as he was on sentry close to the same spot, he was hit, with a round shot which completely shattered his leg. Of course, the leg had to be amputated above where it was hit so as to come at the sinews, and there being no chloroform, the poor fellow could not bear up against his sufferings and expired in great agony.

Another narrow escape from a shell. This to myself. I was one day at an outpost accompanied by the dog as usual, and also a sergeant by the name of Varney. We were looking from loopholes and taking an occasional pot shot at some fellows who were employed in cutting at trenches at some distance from our position. Sometimes we could only see their spades when they threw up the earth. I was just after returning my rifle from the loophole but never shifted my position, when in came a shell, right through the loophole and struck the wall in rear of me and exploded, knocking bricks and mortar about the place. You may be sure I was startled and the dog barking like mad. At last he found me covered all over with bricks and mortar. I looked more like a miller than a soldier. The officer shouted, "Is there anyone hurt?"

The sergeant shouted, "Yes, I think young Metcalfe is killed." for he thought it was impossible to escape.

However, I shouted that I was all right, and when I presented myself I looked such a picture that I was jolly well laughed at. I thought this was rather queer sympathy, but my faithful quadruped showed me plenty as far as licking and pawing went. How I escaped on that occasion I cannot tell. I only had a few scratches from fragments of broken bricks. I suppose the Almighty thought proper to spare me for more hardships.

I will mention an instance of the foolhardiness of some soldiers, and I may say flying in the face of God. We were one day resting after a very heavy night engaged in burying dead battery horses, for fear of sickness arising from the stench caused by them. Well, we were resting, when the cry of "Turn out" made us all start, sick, lame and lazy just as we were, and none too soon, for they were making for the battery.

We had two guns in this battery and one of these was very soon disabled. The other they got off the platform, and we had hard work to get it right again. We had only one artillery man with us for I may say that the greater part of our artillery men were either killed or wounded, so that we had to learn to fire and load the guns ourselves, so that we sometimes found ourselves in the double capacity of artillery and infantry. Well, on this occasion we had only this one man of the artillery. His name was Barry, which bespeaks his nationality. The bullets were whizzing both thick and fast and the men were ducking from them, although when the whiz of a bullet is passed that bullet has passed also, but indeed, he must be a very self-possessed man who will not duck his head occasionally. However, this old artillery man rebuked the lads for ducking so to musket shots. He said you should never duck to anything under a 9 pound shot. While he was going on at this rate a fine young grenadier was shot through the head with a musket ball.

This hardened old gunner made remark— "Ha, that fellow has ducked to musket ball at all events, and" he said, "if ever I am to be killed in action, I hope it will be from a cannon ball and right in the head, so that my death may be soon and sudden."

And indeed his wish was complied with, perhaps sooner than he anticipated, for the next day and at the same hour and the same place, he was accommodated with a round shot right in the head. I need not say his death was soon and sudden.

One more instance and then I will stop and I may say what soldiers are callous to danger and good natured and generous when out of it, perhaps sometimes to a fault. We had a man by the name of Tomlinson who, when he had his allowance of grog no one could stop his tongue from wagging. So much so that he got the soubriquet of "Chatter-box". Well, one day after he had his allowance he must have a look over the parapet to see how his friends the rebels were getting on, and to show your head was the signal to get a bullet through it. Well, this poor individual showed himself and of course received the usual pill in the head, which of course put an end to his career.

Upon this his comrade remarked, "It serves you jolly well right, you confounded ass. I often told you you would be served like that before you were done and my words have come true."

After considering a while and contemplating the corpse of his comrade he burst out crying and said, "Well, I am sorry poor Jack. You were as good a comrade as ever a soldier had," and it was hard to see this generous hearted soldier shed tears. But so it was, from recklessness to tears and from tears back to recklessness again, and so on.

One more. I cannot resist it, and I hope you who read these lines will not take exception to it. It happened in this way. My friend, the Rev Mr Harris, was in the habit of having divine service in the house in which he stayed every Sunday. Indeed, this was about the only way in which we could tell the day of the week, for every day was such a sameness that they all appeared alike to us. Well, on this day Mr Harris came to us and said, "Well now, boys, I am about to have a little divine service, and any of you who wish to join me you will be very welcome to come and attend, and those who don't care to come, I hope you will keep quiet and not disturb us."

Well, we all went, with one or two exceptions. Now, I may state here that the rebels practised all sorts of schemes to alarm the garrison, and amongst them they had recourse to the following. They would dig a hole in the ground with an angle of say 45 degrees. Place some loose gunpowder, then place a great round stone or a great lump of wood on top of this powder, and the angle in which this hole was cut gave this missile whatever it might be, wood or stone, a certain amount of elevation, so that if there was sufficient powder placed in the hole, when ignited it was sure to land in some part of our position, and it would come on with a tremendous whirr and noise that would almost set a person crazy. Well, when Mr Harris was in the midst of his service with his thoughts bent, not on the rebels, but on something more worthy of his calling, one of these interesting bombs, *i.e.* a large block of wood, came whizzing through the air. Just then in rushed a young fellow who had been watching the arrival of this thing. In he rushed into the room where the good chaplain was engaged in prayer, and without the least warning shouted out, "H-y Japers—Boys, the devils are firing cook houses at us." You can imagine the commotion this caused. The man never gave the parson, or what he was engaged in, a thought, but when he realised his position you can imagine his feelings.

About this time another gloom was cast on the garrison by the sad end of a gallant young officer by the name of Birch. This young officer was a lieutenant in one of the Seatapore regiments. I believe his father commanded one of the regiments, and I believe was killed in the mutiny. He had a brother and two sisters in the garrison, and the sisters were continually in the hospital tending on the sick and wounded (like Mrs Nightingale of Crimea fame), and were consequently almost worshipped by the soldiers. [6] This young officer volunteered to reconnoitre the enemies position at night, and orders were given accordingly so that the sentries were to be on the lookout for his return and not to fire on him on his return. I don't know how it happened, whether the order was neglected or what was the case. He was

6. See *Notes* Letter from Brigadier Inglis.

returning by the battery at Gubbins Bungalow, when the sentry, seeing a man outside the position and not knowing who it was, he fired and shot this gallant young officer, and when falling he cried out, "Oh my God, sentry, you have shot me."

The sentry, you may be sure, felt a great shock. He immediately jumped over the parapet and at the risk of his life brought the body of the young officer in to the position. It seems strange that the officer should be fired on by one of his own men, but that is easily explained. We considered that everyone outside our position were enemies, and the fact that we never challenged anyone at night especially, and also the sentry not being apprised of the fact of the officer being out on that occasion, I think you will say that the sentry was blameless which I am sure he was. However, the poor fellow fretted so much over the occurrence that he wasted away to skeleton, and for a long time could not be comforted, and he could never be persuaded to accept of promotion.

As for the corporal whose duty it was to acquaint the sentry of the officer being out, I believe he lost his stripe and met with a sad death years after at the Cape of Good Hope. This family of Birches were very unfortunate. The father killed, the brother killed, and one of the sisters killed with a fragment of an exploded shell when attending on the sick and wounded in the hospital. The younger brother, who was then a young cadet, rose to the rank of major afterwards, and I read was killed when gallantly leading his regiment at the storming of the fort of Al-imessgid (Ali Masjid) in the Khyber Pass during the last Afghan War. I know the place where he fell very well.

And now a little anecdote in connection with an officer of my regiment by the name of McCabe. This was one of the most indefatigable officers in the garrison and one in whom the brigadier placed great confidence, and indeed which was well deserved. This officer was an Irishman and who was promoted from sergeant to a commission for bravery displayed at a former campaign. [7]

7. See *Notes* Letter from Major-General Henry Smith.

Well, this officer was continually bobbing about, as the soldiers termed it, and one night he went outside a certain post and it so happened that an Irishman was on sentry on this particular post, and for fear of another mishap he was made acquainted with the officer being out and likely to pay this man a visit. Well, this soldier was rather hot-tempered, but a good soldier. Nevertheless, the officer was a little hasty also. Well, in came the officer right enough without being challenged, and the spirit of discipline being uppermost, he held forth in the following manner.

Officer "Are you the sentry?"

Sentry answered, "I am, Sir."

Officer "And why the d—— didn't you challenge me?"

Sentry "Because I knew it was you Sir, and that you would be coming this way."

Officer, very severely, "You should have fired, sir. You are not supposed to know anyone outside of your post, especially at night, sir."

Sentry "Then by J—— C—t the next time you will come the same way at night I will accommodate you. I will shoot you right enough."

The officer took no further notice, and did not trouble the same sentry again.

Another about this officer. I was stationed at an outpost called Segoes Bungalow (Sago's House) and was very near the enemy's position, so much so indeed that we could hear them giving and receiving orders. One day there was a severe attack commenced by the enemy blowing up a mine. Two of our men were blown into the road and in the smoke they escaped into the position again. Well, on these fellows came very determinedly, and we had very hard work to keep them out, so much so that I was despatched to this officer for help. I went.

The officer said "Well Metcalfe, what's the matter at Segoes?" meaning the post.

I said, "We are attacked and I am afraid greatly outnumbered, and am sent to you for help."

"Well Metcalfe, I can't afford you any help from my post. We are as bad off as yourselves. Go back and tell your officer that he must keep the post at every risk," at the same time asking me who the officer was and, when I told him, said, "Well, I think I will go with you myself," and indeed that was something for he was really a host in himself and the men thought so much of him that they thought he was as good as twenty men.

However, back we ran as fast as we could. In the meantime our poor fellows were very hard pressed, and on our way he encountered one of the half caste young men on his knees praying away for himself. As soon as the officer saw this, and knowing that the fellow should be helping our men, he gave the poor fellow a cuff in the ear and knocked him off his knees, and said, "What do you mean, you d——d swab. Now is no time for praying when the position is nearly in the hands of the rebels."

We did not wait to see how the poor fellow took it, but scampered on and only just arrived in time. Well, the gallant McCabe was equal to the occasion. He had recourse to a ruse which succeeded admirably. We made such a hubbub in running to the help of our comrades, the officer shouting as if he had a whole regiment with him. He shouted No. 1 will advance, No. 2 support, No. 3 reserve, Charge, as loud as he could, which had the desired effect. I need not say that the enemy waited for the sham charge, but at night we had to be reinforced, for if the enemy found out the ruse, which most surely they would, I am afraid we would have hard work to withstand their attack. However, they did not trouble us afterwards.

And about McCabe, had he lived he would have been made a brevet lieutenant colonel, but it was not to be. Poor fellow. He was mortally wounded leading his fourth sortie. I was with him on the occasion. I believe that when the commander-in-chief heard about him he asked as a favour that he might be allowed to retain his regulation sword as a souvenir of his bravery, for he said there did not exist a braver soldier. The commander-in-chief also recommended that this officer's mother might receive a pension, as this, her son, was the sole means of support, so that being a brave soldier and good officer, he was also a good and dutiful son. His mother got the annuity and if alive is drawing it now, and may she continue to do so.

Well now, Havelock and his brave band are approaching. We hear their firing at Allenbaugh (Alam Bagh), or Allen's garden. We are ordered to be on the alert. All day we are at it, hammer and tongs. This is on the 25th September in the afternoon. Their attacks become more vigorous, the distant cannonading becomes more distinct. The attacks become less frequent. At last we hear the shouts. The most beautiful of sights, we see the head of a column, and at the head rides the bravest of the brave, gallant Havelock, and by his side his gallant and generous comrade Outram.

Oh, what welcome, what joy. Comrades shaking hands, rough soldiers embracing and kissing little ones. Women asking for absent friends etc., but why prolong. Suffice it we are saved, and under God, Havelock was the means, his rapid advance and his glorious entry into Lucknow on the 25th. Had it not been for this, I say that not a man, woman or child of the famous Lucknow Garrison would be alive on the 27th to tell the tale, for the place was thoroughly undermined, the trains laid and everything ready to blow us into the air. This was ascertained after Havelock had been in the Residency a few days, and then and not till then the sad tale of the Cawnpore massacre was verified, and the news caused a sort of reaction, so to speak, in the garrison, for there were a great many who had relatives in Cawnpore.

There was one young lad in the band named Symes. His mother, stepfather, sister and brother were butchered at Cawnpore. I was by when he heard the news. I thought the poor young fellow's heart broke on the spot. However, he made a sort of vow that when he had a chance he would neither spare man, woman or child on account of his family being slain. However, on the morning after Havelock's force came in there were volunteers asked for, to go and clear the position of any of the enemy who were thought to be still in position around us. Well this young lad happened to be of the party, as also myself. After we had been out some time I missed this young fellow. I asked if anyone knew what became of him.

One man told me he had seen him rush into a house close by, pointing to the house. I thought, strange, that the young lad did not come out of the house again, so I made a rush towards the house and I heard a scuffle going on. I rushed in and saw the lad in a very awkward position. A huge sepoy had a hold of the lad's musket and was in the act of cutting at him with his *tulwar*, or native sword. I just arrived in time to save him. He said to me, "Oh, Harry, I am a brute."

I said, "How is that Jack?"

He said, "Oh, I said when I came out I would spare no one, and I fired at a young woman and I am afraid I killed her, and by so doing I have placed myself on a par with the rebels by me killing her. I will not get my own relatives restored to me and consequently I am not fit to be called a soldier or a Christian."

I rallied him on it and said perhaps he had not killed her, but it was no use. I asked him to point out the spot where this took place. He did so, and on going towards the spot we saw some of our men stooping over someone who was laying down. When we got to the spot we found it to be the young woman who the young lad had fired at. She was slightly wounded and had fainted, and in this position our men had found her, and seeing her seemingly all right this young lad almost jumped for joy at the thought of him not killing her. A few men brought this poor young native woman into the garrison and had her wound dressed, and she was then sent about her business, a striking contrast to the way our poor women and children were treated, but then we were soldiers—they were fiends.

Well, this young lad rallied a little and seemed a little more settled, and on our advance we saw a mosque, or native temple, from which temple the rebels had used to keep up an incessant fire on our position. The officer said, "Now lads, we must take this sammy-house at a rush." He placed himself in front, waved his sword. That was enough. The thing was done before we knew where we were, and in overhauling the place we found a quantity of loose powder which I suppose they were about to destroy when we suddenly burst upon them and made them change their plans. We asked the officer to let us destroy it, but he would not allow it without superior authority. Well, this young lad came into the place and without noticing the powder, or perhaps not caring, threw himself down to rest as he felt rather jaded and out of sorts. In the meantime the officer had planted a sentinel at one of the windows to look out, and on the sentry seeing a sepoy running past let fly at him. Well, a portion of the lighted paper was blown into the place where the powder was strewed and where the lad Symes was lying, and the consequence was an immediate explosion. The powder blew up and with it the poor lad, and a frightful spectacle he presented. He was taken in and placed in the hospital, where I remained with him till he died in great agony that night.

I forgot to say that he had two sisters in the garrison, both very respectable young women, and married, one to a colour sergeant, and the other to the drum major. About 10 p.m. the two sisters came to see him. He was then, poor fellow, very low indeed, and the poor sisters, whose husbands were out in the city with a sortie party, and they did not know whether they were dead or alive. I say that seeing these dear sisters talking about their loss at Cawnpore and their dying brother (the last prop of their family), why, it was simply heart rending, so much so that I had to beg of them to leave us and not to embitter the poor lad's last moments. They left, poor things, on my promising to let them know when he was on the point of death.

Well, they left and they had scarcely gone when the poor lad breathed his last. I went to fetch the sisters, and when we got back there was no signs of the remains to be found anywhere. We searched high and low, but no trace could we find. We enquired of the doctors. They could not tell us anything, only they supposed he was taken away to be buried. Well, we started for the graveyard, and it was a beautiful moonlight night, so clear that you could see to pick a pin up, as the saying is, for in India the moon shines with far more brilliancy than at home here in England.

The reason that I mention this was that, strange to say, during our tour round the graveyard not a single shot was fired at us, and at other times you could scarcely show your nose there without having dozens of shots fired at you, so much so indeed that the dead were generally buried under cover of darkness, and you may be sure without much military pomp or ceremony. A few hasty prayers, a few shovels full of earth, and all was done. Well, we could not find what we sought for and so had to retrace our steps to the hospital, for the sisters would not relinquish the hope of having a last farewell look on the remains of their dear brother. At last we found where the remains were deposited. We ran rather than walked and arrived just in time to see two native attendants sewing the remains up in his *guthery*, or native rug.

The sisters wanted to have one more look and natives would not let them because it involved the re-opening of their work and going over the whole thing again. They offered money, but no, they were resolute. At last the sisters appealed to me. I could not withstand the appeal. I asked the natives to let them look. They refused. I then showed them a horse pistol I had with me and said I would blow their brains out if they did not comply. This had the desired effect. They let them look, and I was very sorry after that I got them the privilege, for the scene that ensued I won't attempt to describe. However, I had almost to drag them away, almost more dead than alive, and thus ended this little affair.

Well after Havelock came in, of course he thought he would have nothing to do but withdraw the whole of the force from Lucknow and march back on Cawnpore, but he reckoned without his host. On this account he left all his stores and provisions at Allen Baugh (Alam Bagh) and when he came into us instead of being able to go out he and his force were forced to remain, until finally relieved by Sir Colin Campbell, and consequently reduced our small stock of provisions to one half. [8] Well, you know self-preservation is the first law of nature, and so it was with your humble servant and his faithful dog, who you have

8. See *Notes* Lieut. Edmondstone's Letter.

no doubt lost sight of for some time, and in whom you will be a little interested. You know our very small allowance of food and that small allowance being rendered beautifully less by having more mouths to consume it. You may be sure there would be but a very small amount come to the faithful dog's share, so that I thought, and very reluctantly indeed, the best way out of the difficulty would be to give him back to Mr Harris. So I accordingly brought him the dog and told him that I thought I had fulfilled my part of the compact on account of the dog. I said I thought we had survived the siege and that I had much pleasure in returning the dog to Mrs Harris safe and sound. I did not like to tell him the real cause, but I believe he guessed it. He took the dog back, and by God's help we all survived the siege, Mrs Harris, Mr Harris, Metcalfe and the dog.

But the siege was not over just then. It lasted until finally relieved on the 22nd November by Sir Colin Campbell, and the first thing he did on forming the communication was to send to each man of the beleaguered garrison a small loaf of bread and a dram of grog, both of which I need not say were very much appreciated by us poor half famished wretches. However, before the final relief we had to undergo not a little hardship, what with starvation, sickness, attacks, etc. We had plenty to occupy our time. Indeed, we had no time. I asked a comrade of mine one day how he was getting on.

He said, "All right".

"Why, I heard you were very sick Jim."

"Sick be hanged man, a fellow hasn't time to get sick now".

About the 28th September [9] I was one of some volunteers who were called on to storm a house called Johannas Bungalow. This was a house on the very border of our position, and which we stormed once before and beat the enemy out of it, but owing to our paucity of numbers we were not able to occupy it, and the brigadier thought that after being thrashed out of it once they would not have the cheek to occupy it again, but he was deceived. They occupied it again the same night. I was wounded

9. See *Notes* Lieut. Edmondstone's Letter.

in both legs on this occasion, and the same place happened to be the scene of a little affair which was nearly proving fatal to your humble servant. Those fellows who occupied this place for the second time proved very troublesome to us, and the brigadier determined to make another attempt, and after taking it, to blow the place up with gunpowder. Consequently, volunteers were called for again. Well, I volunteered again, my former wounds being nearly well.

About this time anyway I considered I was all right. Well, there happened to be a great tall soldier of the grenadiers with the party. There were two ladders placed against the two windows, and the word "Forward" was given. We all rushed off together, and whether me being light or small, or what, I reached one of the ladders just as the tall grenadier reached the other, and it was a race between him and me, and although I reached every rung of my ladder as soon as he reached his, still he seemed to be higher than I was, and so he was, and I never allowed for his height. However, I believe he got in at his window before I got in at mine, but when I got in I could not see anyone in my room.

Consequently I concluded that the enemy did not wait for us but took to their heels as soon as we rushed forward. Well, I looked round the room to see if there was anything worth laying hands on in the shape of provisions etc. Well, there was a very large box, something about or nearly resembling a large flour bin. The lid was partly up so I threw it entirely up, and what was my astonishment to see three of my sable friends sitting on their haunches in this big box. Well, I shot one and bayoneted another, but the third was on me like mad and before I knew where I was he had hold of my musket by the muzzle so that I could not use the bayonet at him. So there I was, he chopping away at me with his native sword, and me defending myself the best way I could by throwing up the butt of my musket to protect my head and trying to close with him, which I knew was my only chance. In doing this I received a chop from his sword on the left hand which divided the knuckle and nearly cut off my thumb. Well, he had his sword raised to give me, I suppose, the final stroke, when in rushed the tall grenadier. Tom Carrol took in the situation at a glance and soon put an end to my antagonist by burying the hammer of his musket in the fellow's skull, and when he saw me all covered with blood he shouted out a great hoarse laugh and said, "You little swab, you were very near being done for," and indeed, so I was. I then showed him the box and its contents, and I can tell you it rather astonished him.

I was laid up with my hand for a few days. About a fortnight after this we had another sortie, and that was to try and capture a heavy howitzer from the enemy. Now, there were three of this party who knew the position of this gun. That was a man the name of Ryan, another by the name of Kelly, and myself, and the man who would be first at this gun would be recommended. Well, we all of course would vie for this honour. Well, this Ryan took a circuit on purpose to be first. Well, there was a single brick wall presented itself to us in the way of an obstacle. The other man Kelly knocked the bricks out with the butt of his musket, and as soon as I saw room enough I darted through, and not waiting for anyone I ran off in the direction, never giving it a thought what danger there might be attached to it, and indeed I must admit it was very foolhardy on my part.

Be that as it may, there I got before anyone else and lo, the gun was gone. Well, I had time to scratch my initials of my name in the wheel tracks, left there and got into a yard where the old King kept his game fowl. Well now, I upset two of the baskets that contained the fowl. I got two of them and tied them together before the others came in. Well, I went into a shed and got a chatty full of flour. I emptied this flour into a turban that I had round my cap. A bugler, by the name of King said, "Harry, you had better throw away that flour."

I said, "Why, George?"

"It might be poisoned Harry, you know."

"Poison here or poison there George, I will stick to it. I might as well die of poison as die of hunger."

Well, after all this the officer recommended Kelly as being

the first man at the place where the gun had been, but Kelly manfully enough repudiated the recommendation in my favour (indeed he could do no other) for there was proof positive in my favour, but the recommendation came to nothing then, but perhaps afterwards it did, but I got no cross, which are getting as common as dirt nowadays.

Well, we got back to the garrison about 5 p.m. after taking and blowing up a few places, and when I got in I was asked how much I would take for the fowls. I mentioned some fabulous sum, and the parties were only too willing to give it, but I declined. I gave one fowl to Mrs Harris and the other I gave to a lady who had four or five little ones, and little ones who were reared in the lap of oriental luxury, but who, poor little things, were deprived of them during the siege. To do these people justice they did not want to deprive me of the fowl, but I made them take them, and I have no doubt they enjoyed the morsel, and as for the poisoned flour, I tell you it made about the sweetest bread I thought that ever I tasted, and my comrade nor me, well we were not poisoned.

And with this I will wind up the siege of Lucknow as far as I was concerned. How that was effected I will leave to abler pens than mine. Suffice it we were relieved and the morning after being relieved Sir Colin Campbell ordered our brigadier to parade the whole of his garrison, both blacks, white, and *chicaboos*, and all as we stood. Well, he did so, and such a motley collection of humanity it was never the general's nor anyone else's fortune to look upon. He told the brigadier to parade the 32nd Regiment by itself. He ordered us to close to the left from the remainder, and a sorry sight we looked after deducting the killed, wounded, and sick who were not then able to stand in the ranks. I believe we mustered about 250 of all ranks; that is rather over than under the number, so that you may judge what we suffered during that time, considering we marched into Lucknow on the 27th December, 1856, 950 bayonets, and on the 23rd November '57 we could scarcely muster the 250 mentioned above, and that was exclusive of the depot we left at Cawnpore, which we never saw again.

The general, on beholding what was left of the once gallant 32nd said, "On my honour, Brigadier, you have a motley crowd to command and more like an invalid depot than the once fine regiment who fought with me on the Punjab and on the North-West Frontier, but" he said, "never mind men, you have nobly done your duty and when we get to Cawnpore you shall have a rest to recruit yourselves," but that was easier said than done, and scarcely were his words uttered than a messenger arrived with the intelligence that Cawnpore was once more in the hands of the enemy.

General Windham who was left in charge at Cawnpore attacked the enemy and was defeated by them, and had all his stores and magazine captured from him. This caused a very hasty retrograde movement to be made on Cawnpore, for I may say, at that time to lose Cawnpore would be a very severe matter indeed, for it was considered the key of India, and also the base of the commander-in-chief's operations, so the order was to push on to Cawnpore, a distance of 48 miles, which we covered without a halt, but previous to starting we were startled by the sad intelligence that brave and Christian Havelock was no more. He died through over exertion, and before he realised that the nation had at last conferred on him honours which was well earned by him for previous services, which was denied him and bestowed on individuals less worthy, but such is life. He was buried in the garden of the Allenbaugh, by the comrades whom he so often led to victory. Peace be to him.

We arrived at the Bridge of Boats at Cawnpore and halted for the night. Sent out pickets to line the banks of the Ganges, and the next day we were ordered to advance across the bridge. Our advance was covered by two heavy guns belonging to the Naval Brigade, and a rocket battery. This rocket battery commenced sending rockets into the enemy, which so much confused them that it drew their attention from the bridge, so that the whole force crossed without losing a man, and when we did cross, we very soon cut a passage for ourselves to General Windham and his comrades. We brought all the women and children, sick and wounded with us, and left a force at Lucknow under the command of Sir Jas. Outram to keep the Lucknow mutineers in check. Sir Colin's object was to wait till all the women, children, sick and wounded were sent down the country to safer quarters, then when he got reinforcements he would attack the enemy, and teach them a lesson, which General Windham was not able to do for lack of troops. Indeed, I believe if he had sufficient he would not have suffered the defeat he did, for indeed, whatever people might say to the contrary, and put whatever colouring they could on it, it was a defeat in every sense of the word, and only for the rapid march we made from Lucknow, it was said there would be another massacre at Cawnpore, but thank God, we were the means to prevent.

Well, after the women and children etc. were sent under escort to a safer place, we commenced operations, but previous to their leaving Mr Harris appealed for and obtained leave for me to spend the afternoon of the eve of their departure with himself and wife. I did so and parted with them and my old friend the dog. I forgot to say that the dog had the peculiar name of Bussle. This was about the 30th November, and did not see the dog again until November 1860. Well, my company with others were sent on outpost duty at the Yellow Bungalow. The outpost was composed of one company 32nd, one Company 23rd Welsh Fusiliers, one company 82nd Regiment, one troop 9th Lancers, and two guns R. H. Artillery. Well, the enemy gave us pretty lively times until the afternoon of the 5th December when they showed themselves properly. They came out in great numbers, attacked our pickets, drove in our advanced sentries, and dismounted one of our guns and killing a few of the cavalry horses. We formed up ready to receive them. They pressed us rather hard but we kept our position. They came pretty close to us at one time and it was glorious to see the little troop of 9th Lancers scattering them. An *aide de camp* rode out to our post and said, "Well done men, you will have to keep this post till morning, and then I trust you will not be required to keep it any longer, for on tomorrow it will be our turn to attack." Everyone seemed to be glad to hear this news for we wanted to be at these fellows who had it all their own way for some time back.

Well, while these fellows were attacking our post, Sir Colin with a small force was reconnoitring the enemy's position. They saw him and opened fire on his force from all quarters of their position. This was what Sir Colin wanted, for they showed him the whole of their positions. When he found this out he retired to his camp, and of course the rebels thought they gained a victory, and consequently fired a salute of ever so many guns, and had great feasting in their camp that night, as they thought they thrashed the Verighi dogs again, but they did not know Sir Colin nor what was in store for them the next day. Well, on the morning of the 6th December, the pickets were recalled and we joined our several regiments, and each man was served out with four ounces cooked meat and an allowance of biscuit, by way of a snack before commencing the engagement.

Well, Sir Colin formed one half of his force in three lines with the usual accompaniments of cavalry and artillery. This half was formed on the plain where our pickets withdrew from, and the other half was formed so as to take the enemy in flank. Well, our force advanced and while the whole force of the enemy were opposed to our portion, the other portion dashed in and took the enemy beautifully in the flank and rear, so that Mr Enemy had a rough handling and in less than two hours they were thrashed out of Cawnpore. We dashed into their camp where everything seemed in a state of utter confusion. On that day we recaptured everything the enemy had taken from General Windham besides the whole of the enemy's camp equipage, together with their heavy and light guns, and their treasure and their military stores. We chased them for fifteen miles after taking their camp, and had to march back the same distance the same day, rather stiff work.

It was hot during the day, and when we bivouacked for the night it was very cold. Of course, we were allowed to light fires, and when we lay down beside the fire there was one side of our bodies warm while the other side was freezing, for you must know that it freezes in India in winter, and it being too late at night when we got back to pitch tents. Therefore we had to do without tents, so that we felt the want of them very much, and when it is remembered that we had only a few ounces of biscuit and four ounces of Morocco leather in the shape of beef in our stomach all day, I will leave you to judge how we felt. There was one comfort, we were all alike from the highest to the lowest.

Well, the next morning, which was a beautiful one indeed in more reasons than one, for we expected to have a little rest and relaxation, rose splendidly, and indeed, when we looked round it was a splendid picture to contemplate for when the trumpets and bugles sounded the rouse, what was complete stillness in a second became life and animation and bustle. Well, the grog bugle sounded and each man had an allowance of rum issued to him, and indeed a very welcome guest it was after the cold night. Well, there was no sign of any breakfast for the commissariat had not brought up the rations, and the sailors belonging to Captain Peel had no rum and their captain sent to our colonel to see if we could spare them any. We had only one allowance per man left, and our colonel asked us if we would spare it to the blue jackets, and of course we said we would spare it to them and welcome, and when the sailors heard this, poor gallant tars, they cheered us all over the position.

They asked us how we were off for breakfast. Of course we had none, and they said you shan't be long so, so at it they went and in less than ten minutes there was lumps of beefsteak etc. roasting and frying the best way we could. The fact was the blue jackets chased and killed some of the battery bullocks. I believe some of the sailors cut these bullocks loose for the purpose. However, we had a good breakfast what was a stranger to us for a long time before and sometimes after too, all because the blue jackets got our tot of grog.

After this we were ordered into cantonments for a little rest and breathing, for there was a great deal to be accomplished still. The mutineers were not yet subdued and there was a good deal of hard work and fighting to be got over before we were again masters. Well, as we were marching for our quarters, the general halted the regiment for a short time at the place which was the scene of the atrocious slaughter of our poor companions in arms, and also the poor and defenceless women and children. I won't attempt to describe the scene which followed, for I cannot, the remembrance of it is too sad, and I don't wonder at the Highlanders making the vows that they did, *i.e.* when they came into Cawnpore and when shown the well in which the poor hapless victims were thrown, they knelt down close to the well and took the Highland vow, that for every one of our poor creatures who were thus slain, 100 of the enemy should bite the dust, and I need not say that they kept their vow.

But the Highlanders were not alone in vowing vengeance. The English, Welsh and Paddy Whacks paid the rebels out with the same sauce. We had our Christmas dinner close to this place, and after a little rest we again took the field in company with the Connaught Rangers, under the command of Brigadier Maxwell, with what was called the Flying Column, and well might it be called flying, for we were continually flying from one place to another with an occasional skirmish, that we did not know where we were, at least the fighting machine did not know. Our brigadier was a regular tartar, and we were almost marched to death, but it had to be done and there was very few indeed but kept up with the column, for if you were so unfortunate as to fall to the rear and not able to regain the column again, it was a blue lookout.

However, we found ourselves at last on the Cawnpore or South side of the Grand Trunk Canal, and there we took post so as to keep the Gwalior rebels in check while the commander-in-chief was making his final arrangements for the great attack and final capture of Lucknow. Well, we kept at this work until the 12th March, when we had a sudden order to retire again on Cawnpore and proceed by force march to Lucknow, and it was a force march and no mistake.

We started for Cawnpore about 12 noon, and arrived there

more dead than alive at about 11 at night, were so fatigued that we laid on the ground all night without pitching our tents. We had a rest the next day and the day after proceeded to Lucknow. We arrived there after another long march and took up a position, but had the mortification to hear that we were not to participate in the final capture of Lucknow, us that defended British honour there and when we nearly lost the best part of our regiment. Yes, it was hard. It deprived us of six months *batta* or field pay and another slide on our medal. If we had been a Highland regiment we would be allowed to remain and partake in the attack. Yes, little band, it was hard that you should be deprived of this honour.

After your trials there, which were great
And such as man cannot relate,
When rebel thousands swarm to stand,
To extirpate you from the land,
When Britons power was but a might
And almost vanquished in the fight,
When her struggling powers no aid could render
Your cry was death and no surrender.

Yes, that was the cry and nobly you stuck to it, and for what? To be put out in the cold, when honour was to be gained, for it must be remembered we stood alone in Lucknow, shut out from the world from the 30th June till reinforced by General Havelock, and the only excuse for this treatment was that Cawnpore was threatened again by the Nana and the Gwalior contingent. Well, we marched again for Cawnpore. You will say that we would have Cawnpore on the brain by that time. If we had not it on the brain we had it pretty well in the feet. However, there was no help for it but grumble and go, and when we reached our destination there was grumbling loud and long.

We landed and parted from the 88th and jolly glad we were too, for although a finer lot of fellows for fighting you could seldom excel, yet their colonel, who was the brigadier, was very severe and would not care if the regiment marched to the Antipodes so that he could be accommodated with a little fighting. Of course, these great guns get the least of the fighting, and the lion's share of the prize money, and the rank and file the greatest share of fighting and the scantiest portion of prize money.

For the defence of Lucknow my regiment was made Light Infantry and a small brass ornament to wear in our caps. We got one year's service without pay and the black sepoys who remained faithful to us all got promotion and three years' service with the order of merit and pay. Mark the distinction.

After a rest. we had the order to proceed to Allahabad, and remained there for a short time, when we were ordered with a small force of horse artillery and cavalry to a place called Ghoophy Ghange (Gopi Ganj?), where an indigo planter had been surrounded by rebels and his life threatened. He held out manfully against these fellows until they heard that we were advancing to his relief, when they bolted, not however, before they destroyed and burned his property, which was rather extensive, and the enemy made the mistake of running foul of us and a short skirmish ensued which did not last very long, for when they found out their mistake they scattered in every direction, not however, before a good many of them bit the dust. This was a very hot day, and I got a touch of sunstroke, but it was dealt with in time so that I did not suffer much. I was able to march back to Allahabad the next day, and on the 12th July '58 we crossed the Ganges in boats to proceed to the relief of the 54th regiment who were hard pressed at a place called Seram. Remained in standing camp there till about the 1st August when we were threatened by the enemy.

Our brigadier marched about 10 miles to a place called Dhini where the enemy were strongly posted in an entrenched position. He reconnoitred, and in doing so was pretty well fired on by the enemy. He retired on Seram our camp, and the next morning advanced with the whole of his force, except a detachment left in the camp for protection. Well we arrived at our destination about seven or eight o'clock, and as smart an engagement for the time it lasted did not take place during the whole campaign. Before 10 o'clock the whole of the position were in our hands, together with the whole of their guns, stores, and ammunition, and what escaped of the enemy were scampering over the plain in every direction, followed by our cavalry and horse artillery. We remained there the remainder of the day, destroying the works and in the cool of the evening we marched back to camp, and thus ended the battle of Dhini with very little loss on our side, a few wounded and one man of the 54th killed. This man was one of the party who was detailed to guard the camp, but he took the place of another man who was married and had a family, and thus, poor fellow, met his death. After this action I was promoted corporal.

Present at the bombardment and capture of the fort of Thyrrool on the 15th August '58. We marched about fifteen miles to attack this fort. We were hammering away at it for two days and on the morning of the third took the place by storm. Took the whole of their guns on this occasion, marched back to camp, and our colonel gave each man a glass of grog, and because the quartermaster had not the grog up at once to be issued to the men, he abused the quartermaster very much. He was a man who thought a great deal of his men, and did not like to see them neglected.

After this we had a month's rest and then broke up camp and marched to join the commander-in-chief's army at a place called Sultanpore. We were here some time, and the enemy appeared in force at a place called Doudpore. (The places in India are nearly all poors or bads.) We were ordered out to smash them. We did so and I shall never forget it. On the night before the action I put on a new pair of Wellington boots (boots could be purchased very cheap in India). Well, I put these boots on and we were told we would start very early in the morning so that we could get the action over and get back again to camp before the sun would attain a very high altitude. We were told we would have to go about five miles, thrash them, and be back again. We started in the morning, me keeping the new boots on all night so that I might have no trouble in putting them on in the morning.

Well at the end of the five miles we halted and sent out *videttes*, but no enemy were to be seen. A spy came in and informed the general that the enemy were about three miles in advance, strongly posted in a beautiful position, and indeed they were, but the three miles turned out to be nearer eight. Be that as it may, away we went for them. After being marching some time we came to a very dense jungle and my regiment were ordered to skirmish through it. I forgot to mention that my regiment was partly filled up from home by this time by drafts sent out to us.

Well, we skirmished through this jungle. Sometimes we could not see our right or left files, and indeed our front rank men (I was in the rear rank). Well, we got out of this at last and formed up on what appeared at first sight a beautiful plain, but when we got into it and the action commenced, I thought we got into a pretty puddle, for the beautiful plain, as we thought, turned out to be a large field of rice, where the natives had been inundating with water from wells, and when we got into it and the enemy commenced peppering us with grape and round shot I thought a great many of us would bite the dust before we got out of it. Every step we took we would sink ankle deep and more sometimes.

Meantime the cavalry and horse artillery (splendid arm of the service) got up on our flanks and it took them a long time to come up for they could not get through the jungle the same as the infantry, and when they came up and commenced operations the enemies fire was drawn from the infantry. Well, we got out of the mud after a while and went in with the bayonet, headed by our gallant Colonel Carmichael. It was a grand sight to see him. Like a giant he was, about 6 ft. 2½, and built in proportion. We, I mean the infantry, turned the enemy's flank and they soon showed the back seams of their jackets, and the cavalry and the R.H.A. completed the game. The infantry were called off and highly complimented by the general, and they well deserved it, for their advance through morass and the enemy peppering them all the time, their steadiness and coolness deserved all praise. The cavalry and artillery also deserved great praise which they got on their return.

Well, we were served, each man, with a tot of grog, and ordered to lay down under the shade of the trees for the morning's fatigue was too much for the infantry to march back again after the action. We remained under the trees for a considerable time, and I fell asleep, and these beautiful boots that was flide-de-flop on my feet when we were going through the mud of rice field were many degrees too big for my feet, (for country leather will stretch when wet, it not being properly tanned). When the sun got at them when I was asleep they shrank up again so that I could scarcely move in them, as hard as they could possibly be.

When the bugle sounded the fall in I rose up, and Oh, such a stinging headache. I thought my head would burst, and those beautiful boots made matters worse. I thought I should never reach camp, and indeed, I wished a friendly bullet would find its billet in my then miserable body. I could not help it, for I really was bad, and still so bad I would not give in and be carried on the elephant which we captured from the enemy, though frequently urged to do so by the officer and comrades, for I believe they were sick of looking at me in my misery. No, I would not give in. I believe my stubbornness kept me up on that occasion.

At length a halt was called, and Oh with joy I heard the sound. I believe I hailed that sound with more joy than the remainder did the sound of the subsequent sound for grog, and that is saying a great deal. As soon as we halted I asked one of my comrades to cut off my enemies (the beautiful boots). "Nonsense Harry, if you do you won't be able to march to camp."

I said never mind, do as I tell you. He did so and after I got my allowance of grog and a little rest I was ready for the road again. We were then about seven miles from camp. A nice job for bare feet, which were already sore enough, but I did it, and I afterwards heard my comrades say that it was as good as a pantomime to watch me picking soft parts of the road to walk upon.

I did it however, and got back all right, but how I felt the next morning I will not say.

On arriving in camp we were served with an allowance of grog, and the captain of my company asked me how I felt. I told him I did not know. He said could you do with another allowance of rum, and I said I thought I could, and he gave it to me and he remarked that I was the most persevering little man he ever knew. He asked me why, when I felt so bad, that I did not give in. I said if I did my comrades would laugh, and it was. I was too proud to wear the ordinary soldiers' boots. I must needs wear Wellington's, going into action, but I said, I would never wear Wellington's again, and indeed I have kept my word, for they are rather too expensive out of India.

"Well," the officer said, "What became of the Wellington's?"

I said I had thrown them away. He then gave me what would have bought two pairs of Wellington's, and thus ended the action of Doudpore on the 14th November 1858. After a short time the commander-in-chief ordered a flying column commanded by our colonel, Colonel Carmichael. We had pretty nice times with him, long and frequent marching certainly, but he never worried us and we worked hard for him so (getting) him his C.B. which he got subsequently, and he richly deserved it. Well, on one occasion we marched all one day from 5 a.m. till 7 p.m. We saw the enemy several times but they would not stay to engage. I think they were getting tired, and indeed so were we, but we had to finish the work cut out for us, *i.e.* put the mutiny down before we were done and we did it. Well, we got to the banks of the Gogra River.

Our object was to keep the enemy in check and from crossing the river until the chief came upon them. Well, when the enemy heard there was a force at the river they changed their tactics and broke ground. Well, when the chief heard this he ordered our force to change also, and march to Deriabad (a bad again). Well, off we started, and got within five miles of the place when an orderly mounted on a swift camel overtook us. We were ordered to the right about at once, and march back to the Gogra. We got there just in time, for the enemy, when they found we were gone, started back for the place they left, which was the easiest part of the river for fording. They were just about to cross when we got up and when we opened fire they were taken properly by surprise, and were thinking about retiring when up came the chief with his army. The job was very soon finished. He took the whole of the rebel camp, stores, guns, treasure, elephants, and several thousand prisoners, which surrendered unconditionally, but the head vagabond got off.

The general was employed the whole of that day in sending the captured stores across the river, and the next day crossed himself and his force, and when passing our camp we were turned out to cheer him, but instead of us cheering him he ordered his army to halt and gave us three cheers, which of course we responded to. That night we received a general order, the commander-in-chief expressing his thanks at our rapid force march and the way we handled the enemy at the banks of the Gogra, but that did not pull up for being deprived of the honour of being present at the fall of Lucknow. However, he gave us an easy job, and ordered us to go with the commissioner collecting all the arms from every village.

We were employed in this .work until the beginning of March 1859, which was a very easy job indeed, comparatively speaking. Sometimes march ten miles, sometimes five, and so on according to the distance from village to village, so that we had a very easy time indeed. I must say it was marred by a few instances of cruelty. Some people would call it cruelty, and indeed I must coincide with those, for whatever might occur in the heat of action there is some excuse for, but flogging natives because they denied all knowledge of where the arms were hid, I cannot agree with. Whenever the commissioner went to a village he demanded to see the head man of the said village. He would then demand the amount of and description of arms in their village. On their denying all knowledge concerning them, they were brought to camp and flogged till they acknowledged, which they might have done at first and saved their back. I believe this was necessary as it saved these districts from joining in any more mutinous conduct.

However, this wound up the campaign as far as my regiment was concerned, and very glad we all were when we got the order to march into Allahabad, there to be broken up previous to proceeding to Old England once more, and on the 10th March 1859 the regiment was broken up to give volunteers for those regiments remaining in India, every soldier who volunteered to any regiment remaining in the country and medically fit got a bounty of thirty *rupees* = to £3 English. We had a good many remain behind, especially young soldiers who joined at the far end of the campaign and who were prevented by some cause or casualty from taking part in much of the fighting. I had to remain behind at Allahabad after the regiment proceeded on its journey down country to escort a man who was tried for theft. I believe he and some others broke into the treasury at Allahabad while his regiment was at the front.

The treasury was robbed of several thousand *rupees*. This fellow was caught and tried, and sentenced to be flogged and some imprisonment. I forget how much, but I believe he never done it, for he on the regiment landing, deserted, and was never heard of afterwards, and a good job, and would have brought disgrace on the regiment, whose name was spotless before that scoundrel came to it, for be it understood that he was not one of the Lucknow heroes, but one who came from England in a draft of recruits who joined us. I believe he had a blank discharge from the marines and at that time the authorities were glad to get any sort of man to fill up the gaps caused by the bullet and pestilence.

The headquarters of my regiment embarked for England on the 22nd March 1859. They landed on the 12th September 1859. The company that I belonged to was not to accompany the headquarters, for there was not sufficient room. We were destined to go in another. Fatal destiny for some. The officer commanding my company was to command detachments of different regiments proceeding in this ship, consisting of the left wing of the 84th Regiment, the 2nd Battalion Military Train, and H. Coy 32nd Regiment, the company I belonged to. We embarked on the 17th April and were towed out to sea on the 19th and 20th and on the evening of the 17th there was one of the ship's company sent ashore from the ship for refusing to work or sail in the ship, for he swore there was cholera in the ship, which was only too true.

The cholera did break out in the ship and the boatswain of the ship was the first who was attacked and died. The ship's cook was the next, but he got over it. It next broke out amongst the troops, and it was— well, you may imagine that fell disease breaking out in a crowded ship of somewhere about eleven or twelve hundred tons burden, and about 500 men and women on board, exclusive of the ship's company. Why, it beggars description. I would go through the siege of Lucknow again sooner than experience the same, for in Lucknow, what with the excitement from shot and shell, and mines, etc., as the man said, there was scarcely time to get sick, and there was an end of it, but this way we were cooped up in a dirty ship. Bear in mind this was not one of H.M.'s troopships, but an old tub of a merchant ship that was hired in a hurry for the occasion, for there was so many troops coming home from India at that time that they were glad to get any sort of a tub to transport troops in, and as for the crew, well, the less said about them the better, only they were composed of all sorts.

Well, the cholera continued to make havoc, throwing overboard every day at the rate of four and five, till the ship had to lay to at the Sand Head and the General Doctor signalled for from Calcutta. He came, and previous to his coming the troops were ordered to bring everything from the troop deck up to the main deck; give the ship a thorough overhauling from stem to stern as the saying is, and then disinfected. All the men who were suffering at the time were taken up and placed under an awning on the poop. The pumps were set to work, salt water pumped into the ship and pumped out again, and it is almost impossible to conceive the filth that was got out of the ship. However, by the time the General Doctor came on board the ship had assumed a pretty tidy appearance, and when he did come on board and saw the arrangements he said we could not have done better if we were trying for a twelve month and told us, that the only chance we had was by proceeding on our voyage.

And now for a couple of instances in connexion with this disease. There was on board an old sergeant major who belonged to the company's service and whose term of service had expired. He was pensioned off from the service and was homeward bound to rest after his well earned pension—for in those days if a man enlisted in the company's service you had to remain in India the whole of the time that would entitle you to a pension and that would be the whole term of 21 years. Well, this man had no doubt been the whole of that time there and you would say long enough too. Well, when the General Doctor was about to step into his boat which was to take him to his steamer, this sergeant major went to him and said, "Will you kindly allow me, Sir, to go back to Calcutta in your steamer? I don't wish to remain any longer aboard this plague-stricken ship."

The General Doctor stared at him (and well he might) for such a strange request. He said, "My good man the only chance you have is to go on in your ship."

The man said, "The only chance I have is to accompany you back to Calcutta and that I'll do right or wrong."

He tried to persuade him but it was no use. At last the doctor said to him, "I think you are afraid."

The man said, "You have just hit it. Sir, I have been in many a rough scene and many a bloody engagement and never felt the least dread or uneasiness till now."

And I believed that man. However the General Doctor humoured him and took him in his boat and, as he was descending the ship's side the doctor made the remark, "I believe he has it now—and sure enough before the steamer was out of sight the signal was made from her mast head that this man had died. Such is the force of fear. I believe that man would have faced the cannon's mouth in action without the least hesitation and often done so, yet acknowledged his fear of the cholera and I have not the least hesitation in saying that fear was the cause of his death."

And now for an opposite character. Whatever you may say of this, and I know you will stare, for it is enough to make anyone stare. We had an old soldier belonging to my company whose name was Roberts. It was his duty to look after the arm chest and keep the rifles and bayonets etc. in order. One day he was doing something with the chest, the ship giving a sudden lurch the chest got on his foot somehow and bruised his great toe. Well this poor old soldier took the cholera and when the orderlies were rubbing the cramps in his legs, his constant cry was, "Oh mind my big toe!"

Well it came to the turn of a hardened individual to be over poor Jack Roberts and of course the usual cry of "Oh mind my big toe." Well, this wretch put up with the cry a good while and indeed I must give him the credit of doing his duty by this poor man. The sweat was pouring off him in streams, he rubbed so hard.

Just now this poor fellow shouts, "Oh Martin mind my big toe," when, "Oh," the hardened wretch shouts, "d—— your B—— big toe what the —— will you do when you get cramp in your old toe?"

So much for him. Anyway the poor man did not suffer much longer.

And now I am going to wind up the cholera question with a dog story (you see the dogs will be in it). I mentioned two young women whose brother was blown up with gunpowder and their stepfather, their brother and sister and their mother were killed at Cawnpore. Well, one of those two young women was courted by our drum major and when the depot was left at Cawnpore this young man left his sweetheart a pet dog by way of a keepsake. Well, after we had been at Lucknow for some time, this young drum major applied for and obtained leave to proceed to Cawnpore and marry this young girl. He went there and got married, brought his wife to Lucknow thus saving her from massacre but the dog was left to her sister at Cawnpore. I may say this sister was left a widow as her husband was one of the victims of the cholera on march.

Well, this dog it seems escaped from the trenches at Cawnpore and when our women from the residency got to Cawnpore this dog by some means found its way to the place where the women were in camp and immediately recognised its old mistress and jumped on her. You may be sure this act on the part of the faithful quadruped awakened up old scenes and associations, some joyous no doubt and others—well we shan't dwell on them. Suffice she got the dog and also obtained readily a free passage in our ship. The captain said he could not refuse it and indeed he said he was rather glad to have to say that he not only brought home some of the Lucknow heroes but brought something which escaped from the trenches at Cawnpore. You will scarcely believe but the dog took sick. Everyone said it showed every symptom of the cholera.

Be that as it may the poor brute in a very short time died and was very soon food for fishes and I will say that there was a general sorrow, so to speak, for the faithful animal was becoming a great favourite. Strange to say that we had not one case after that, and we were beginning to look up a bit and singing "Home Sweet Home" again when about four nights after this we were all surprised to hear that a fine young soldier of the military train was taken suddenly ill, and died with a few hours sickness. He was a troop sergeant major and much respected by all hands. He was all through the Crimean Campaign including the Balaclava charge of the Light Brigade and through the Indian Mutiny including the relief and capture of Lucknow, and to die thus and become food for fishes. The sailors say it's a glorious death. Give me the tented field. But such is life and truly might it be said in the midst of it we are in death.

But enough, we are homeward bound and all of a sudden we get wind bound and are knocking about the Andaman and Knickabu (Nicobar) Islands in what the sailors call the Doldrums, that is neither going backwards or forwards. Well we find ourselves suddenly abreast of one of these islands on a Sunday morning and the captain ordered the ship to be hove to. We had not been long in this position before we saw a good many canoes putting off to us manned by fine stalworth fellows almost nude. There was one old dignified gent stood up in the stern of his canoe and in plain English hailed us with— "Ship Ahoy— What ship is that?"

Ans. "The *Pomona* of Liverpool."

Ques. "Then where are you bound for?"

Ans. "England."

Ques. "What's your cargo?"

Ans. "Live lumber: *i.e.* Soldiers."

Ques. "Do you want any more?"

Ans. "What have you got?"

Ans. "Pigs."

Captain— "Come alongside."—and alongside they come.

The captain said to the native in the stern "Who are you?"

"I am the King of the Island."

"Will you come on board?"

"Yes." He steps on board and a card he was. He had something around his loins and something on his head. When he came on board the captain offered him an old gun which was in use in Queen Ann's time and he got two beautiful grunters for it. I offered him a few *rupees* for one for my mess but he refused. The colour sergeant tried him with an old rusty clasp knife and succeeded. You may imagine what a hunt ensued for old knives and forks after that but the remainder were all bought up by the captain for the officer's table and two others he kept and sold them at Gravesend for a good price.

After the captain had done with the pig business the officers dressed up this sprig of Royalty in a scarlet jacket, a pair of white small clothes, top boots and an old silk hat. They then placed him in front of a mirror and the capers that ebony faced individual cut were sublime. He did not know himself and he danced about the poop deck like a maniac, which he was not far removed from one, and his gesticulations to his men in the boat were something grand. It was to one of these Islands that the old King of Delhi was transported after being captured after the fall of Delhi for his complicity in the mutiny. It was here also that Lord Mayo was assassinated by one of the natives who was transported to there, when he Lord Mayo was there on an official visit.

Sailors say that if you only wait for a fair wind you will be sure to get it and so did we, one which sent us spinning out of the Doldrums and away from the Islands but before getting clear of the Bay of Bengal a squall suddenly struck the ship and threw her on her beam ends. That means that our yards were touching the water on one side, and one of our soldiers more wise in his generation than his comrades, shouts out, "Come all you fellows to this side to balance the ship."

A very wise suggestion—by the way, since we got out of that scrape without any casualty worth speaking of and never lost a brace or a tack till we came off the Cape of Good, rightly called the Cape of Storms. We sighted Tabel Bay about 3 p.m. on the 1st July and it was three days before we could get into port. We wanted to run in here to get a fresh supply of provisions and water. The latter was the most needed as we seemed very short. We got supplied and it was fourteen days before we could get out again. When we got out we got a fair wind which lasted till we arrived in the chops of the Channel. I may add that we had the 2nd anniversary of the relief by Havelock, *i.e.* the 25th Sept., and there being a good few of Havelock's Heroes on board, the 84th Regt, our commanding officer ordered an extra allowance of grog to the troops and ships company about 5 p.m., about the time that Havelock's force got to the Residency of Lucknow, and you may be sure that this was the cause of many an incident in connection with the occasion to be talked over and battles and skirmishes being fought over again and messing comrades called to mind, their good qualities talked over and extolled and their bad ones if any never alluded to.

We anchored in Gravesend Reach on Saturday October 11th, 1859 and the next morning Sunday were awakened by the welcome and beautiful sounds of the different bells. Calling the inhabitants to early worship. The tones of these bells were the sweetest music that we heard for many a year and were doubly so to us who were cooped up in an old tub of a transport ship for nearly six months, on the eve of our leaving her for *terra firma* on the morrow, all being well. And we disembarked on Monday and took a train for Dover midst the shouts and acclamations of the inhabitants of Gravesend. I may also state that when the rest of the ships in the harbour found out who were on board our ship their crews manned yards and gave us three splendid cheers, such cheers as only can be given by British tars.

Well, we arrived at Dover about 3 p.m. on 13th Oct. and our reception there was no less cordial than the ovation which was accorded us at Gravesend. There were no less than three military bands playing us from the station to the barracks to the old air "See the Conquering Heroes Come," etc. The streets and windows were beautifully decorated with flags, banners, etc. with the words displayed here and there "Welcome The Heroes of Lucknow—Welcome the Protectors of Women & Children" & etc.

This was all very nice and grand and gratifying to the war-worn soldier and gave us to understand that we were not forgotten by a grateful public for our services. And so it would be if the same feeling always remained but our deeds like everything else were soon forgot by that grateful public and by others also, and of course gradually drifted into the common soldier once more, till our grateful country once more required the services of those forgotten (and in some instances I am sorry to write) despised ones. Such is the soldier and such is the grateful public also. Indeed I might quote here the lines of a once famous commander who says—

When war is proclaimed and dangers nigh
God and our soldiers is the peoples cry
But when peace is proclaimed and all things righted
God is forgot and the soldier slighted.

And I can safely say it is a fact. I obtained a furlough and went home and soldier-like fell courting very fast and at the expiration of my furlough came back and left the girl I loved behind me, but not like most soldiers for good, for in six months time I went back and married the girl I left behind me and we have not parted company since. And soon after came back to the regiment who were stationed in Aldershot where I was promoted to the rank of sergeant.

And now about the Lucknow dog again. I said I left the dog with Mr Harris after Havelock's relief. I saw him only once after that and that was when I went to take leave of Mrs and Mr Harris previous to them proceeding down country. That would be about the end of Nov. '59. I did not see him again until one day about the beginning of November 1860 when I was on what they term line duty at the permanent barracks at Aldershot and just as I faced inwards towards the block, who should I see running towards me but Mr Harris accompanied by the dog who the moment he saw me immediately recognised me and commenced jumping at me and cutting all sorts of joyful antics. Now this seems rather strange after a laps of three years that the dog should know me again but he did. Mr Harris came with the express purpose of obtaining leave for my wife and me to spend the next day with him and some friends of his.

He got us a cab and we spent a very enjoyable day and after lunch I was rather surprised when Mr Harris returned after a short absence with a very big pipe indeed and a great paper of tobacco and he said, "Now Metcalfe, if I could not accommodate you in Lucknow, I can now"; handing this great long pipe and the tobacco, and now he said, "Smoke till you are black in the face," and indeed I paid attention to it. Our reception on that occasion was good indeed and well worthy the lady and gentleman who accorded it, and on that occasion he renewed his promise to me that he made on a former occasion but I never saw him after that and I am almost ashamed to own that I never corresponded with him.

Well, after remaining in Aldershot till August '61 we got the rout to Plymouth, was there when the Prince Consort died and also when the Prince of Wales was married, when all the arrangements were carried out in a splendid state both afloat and ashore. We left Plymouth for Ireland on the 14th April 1863, were stationed at the Curragh Camp, a splendid place for exercising large bodies of troops. Marched for Richmond Barracks, Dublin on the 10th October '63. Went to the school of Musketry, Fleetwood, Lancashire on the 15th April for the purpose of studying for the post of Musketry Instructor. I was there till the 1st September. I was at Wimbledon at the great meeting of 1864 when a drill sergeant of the Guards shot a marker. Joined the regiment again from Fleetwood after obtaining my certificate of qualification. The regiment marched back to the Curragh again during my absence at Fleetwood, so I joined them there again.

We marched from there to Waterford and Kilkenny, one half of the regiment stationed at each place. My company went to Duncannow, where I had a son born to me on Xmas day of 1864. Went back to the Curragh again in March 1865 and on the 5th July embarked on board H.M. Ship *Himalayah* for conveyance to Gibraltar and disembarked on the 12th July. Previous to our disembarkation my eldest child Agnes was severely scalded by upsetting a tin pot of boiling tea on herself but thank God she got over it all right. I was put on the public works in Gibraltar and had charge of 150 men but of course under the superintendence of the Royal Engineers. Our friend the cholera paid us another visit at Gib and the troops suffered most severely here while it lasted and your humble servant was not an exception to the rule on this occasion for I got an attack of it here too, but thank God, as in the first, I was granted a longer day. We lost a good many men here, one woman and several children. I was nearly losing my eldest girl, Agnes, but she was spared and after this my Christmas box was very near going but he was also spared thank God. I was here appointed canteen sergeant for six months and at the expiration of my term was promoted colour sergeant of a company.

In May '67 we got the route for the Mauritius, formerly called the Isle of France. Well, we embarked on board H.M.S. Ship

Orontus and arrived at Simons Bay, Cape of Good Hope, where stayed for a short time owing to an epidemic which broke out in the Mauritius among the native coolies who were suffering very much from it. At last we steamed for the Mauritius and arrived at Port Louis on the 3rd July 1867 and disembarked the next day, 4th July. A small detachment was left at Port Louis and the remainder with headquarters proceeded to Mayhburgh (Mahebourg) and remained there until February 1868 and during our stay here I was presented with another increase. On the 14th Sept. a daughter was born to me and on the following February we embarked at Port Louis on board H.M. Ship *Urgent* for the Cape of Good Hope where we arrived after ten days steam and disembarked at East London.

After being in camp for a few days we marched for Fort Beaufort on the frontier. We marched to King William's Town and were well received by the regiment lying there at the time, H.M.'s Holy Boys. [10] After resting here a few days we started for Fort Beaufort and after four days march arrived at that station. Very easy times at this place. We remained here till November 68 and then got the route for Graham's Town which was the headquarters for the Eastern Province. I was appointed Garrison Sergeant Major at Port Elizabeth and remained here my own master for a considerable time. While I was stationed here I witnessed a terrific storm, the wind blowing from the south east. There were nineteen ships wrecked, and one of these ships was totally smashed to pieces and all hands lost and this in sight of thousands who could render them no assistance. I remained at Port Elizabeth until 1871 when I was ordered to rejoin the left wing of my regiment which was stationed at King William's Town.

This was rather unexpected for I was drawing my weeks allowance of fuel about 12 noon and was on board the mail steamer bound for East London again at 4 p.m. Rather quick work and which caused me to part with a good many articles at a great sacrifice. However, there was no help for it. I had to grin

10. The Royal Norfolk Regiment.

and bear it. We arrived at East London all right after a very nice run of two days and disembarked the same day and marched again for King William's Town where I remained till November 1871 when I passed the Board of Claims and retraced my steps once more to East London, there to embark once more for England.

And now once more we are homeward bound. My services in the regular army would expire on the voyage home. We embarked again at East London, called in at Simon's Bay where the soldiers and ships company had great fun in catching fish. We sailed from there and had Christmas off the Island of St. Helena, the grave of that once famed Napoleon. Next called at the Island of Ascension, so called through being discovered on Ascension Day. We coaled here and proceeded on our voyage, next called at St. Vincent, after that crossed the Bay of Biscay which was very stormy, but our ship rode through it like a duck. We arrived at Queen's Town after a beautiful passage. Our next place was Plymouth where we took in Supernumeraries for the Channel Fleet which we left at Portland.

Our next and final stage was Portsmouth and on the 29th January 1872 we landed and proceeded by rail to Chichester, the discharge depot, where I remained a few months as clerk in the discharge office, when I was discharged and joined the East York Militia at Beverley, Yorkshire, as Musketry Instructor, where I remained for three year and six months and after being thoroughly disgusted with the militia I purchased my discharge and joined the 27th Cheshire Rifle Volunteers at Wilmslow. There I thought I would remain and settle down after many roving years but it was not to be. After being there about four years where I was nicely settling down, my commanding officer, in acknowledgement of my services, promoted me to the post of senior instructor to the Macclesfield Volunteers. This was to better my position and so it did in a monetary sense but I was much happier where I was.

Notes

1. From a letter written by Major-General John Edmond-stone, 32nd Light Infantry, when a Lieutenant in his Regiment after the Siege of Lucknow in 1858:—

Cawnpore. 4th January, 1858.
My dearest Mother,
For the last three or four days I have been lying on my back from a severe attack of rheumatism; so bad it was, that I lost the power of moving the lower part of my body, but I am almost all right again just in time to write you a short letter as the mail goes out this afternoon. I will give you a short sketch of my proceedings.
On the 30th of June as you know the fatal battle of Chin-hut took place; I was not out there, but was sent but with thirty-eight men to cover the retreat, by holding the Iron Bridge, which I did for a long time under a very heavy fire of musketry, but by putting my men down in a good position I had only one killed and one wounded.
The enemy forded the river in order to cut us off in the rear, when I sent in to know whether I was to retire, or hold the position at all risks. I was immediately recalled and told we had done good service, it was rather ticklish work, being out on my own responsibility, and being the first time I was ever under fire. A young boy of the 41st N.I. Ensign McGregor went out with me as a volunteer and right well did he behave, poor fellow he is since dead.

2. Lieut. Edmondstone's letter continues:— ,

The next night about 11 o'clock, I was sent for, by Sir Henry Lawrence, to occupy a mosque with fifteen men to cover the retreat of the Muchie Boun party, the retreat was effected without a shot being fired and I withdrew my party very glad to do so as I certainly expected desperate work.

3. In her diary *(A Lady's Diary of the Siege of Lucknow,* John Murray, 1858) Mrs Harris writes:—

July 4th 1857. A soldier of the 32nd, called Metcalfe, has taken charge of dear old Bustle for us. He was so much in the way down in the Tye Khana, and received such black looks from —— and ——, we were afraid we should have been obliged to condemn him to death as the most merciful way of getting rid of him, when this delightful man, who is on guard at this house, offered to take charge of him for us till better days should come.

4. Lieut. Edmondstone's letter again:—

After that we had fearful work, turned out twice or thrice every night. My station was the Redan battery one day, and the gorge of the Redan the next. Laurence with the light company took turn about with me. On the 20th of July I was at the gorge of Redan when that desperate attack took place, my company was divided into three parties so I had to move about a good deal; when standing at the mortar of Macfarlane's (Mrs Young's friend) battery I got shot in the stomach; so little pain it was I did not think it had entered, it was just as if a hard ball had struck me, it took my wind away, not hearing the ball drop and not finding it in my clothes I thought it would be advisable to go to hospital and see what sort of wound I had got. Directly I undid my belt I got quite sick. I found the ball had run along under the muscles of the stomach for about seven inches where it was cut out. I was in hospital about a month four pieces of cloth having remained in the wound which made it troublesome.

After I was discharged and at my duty, the wound broke out again and I had to go to hospital for another week then I came out and was at my duty for a fortnight but was very ill all the time with low fever, after walking ten yards I used to go quite blind and have to sit down till my sight came again. I was obliged to go into hospital again and did not come out till the 27th September, two days after Havelock came in. I was so thin that when I weighed in the butchers scales I was only 8st 11 lbs, rather a come down from 11st 5 lbs."

5. Letter from Colonel Inglis commanding the Residency Garrison, to General Havelock:—

25th August.

My dear General,

Lest my letter of the 16th should have miscarried I send herewith a duplicate of its contents a note from Colonel Tytler to Mr. Gubbins reached last night dated Mungal-war 4th inst. The latter paragraph of which is as follows. 'You must aid us in every way even to cutting your way out if we cannot force our way in. This has caused me much uneasiness as it is quite impossible with my weak and scattered force that I can leave my defences. You must bear in mind how I am hampered, that I have upwards of 120 sick and wounded and at least 220 women and 180 children and no carriage of any description besides sacrificing twenty-three *lakhs* of treasure and about thirty guns of sorts.

In consequence of the news I shall soon put the force on half rations unless I hear again from you. Our provisions will last us then till about 10th September. If you hope to save this force no time must be lost in pushing forward. We are daily being attacked by the enemy who are within a few yards of our defences. Their mines have already weakened our post and I have every reason to believe they are carrying on others. Their eighteen pounders are within 150 yards of some of our batteries and from their position and our inability to form working parties we cannot reply to them and therefore the damage done hourly is very great. My strength now in Europeans is 350 and about 300 natives, and the men dreadfully harassed, and owing to part of the Residency having been brought down by round shot, many are without shelter. Our native force having been assured on Colonel Tytler's authority of your near approach some 25 days ago, are naturally losing confidence, and if they leave us I do not see how the defences are to be manned. Since the above was written the enemy have sprung another mine.

General Havelock had already written to Colonel Inglis who had evidently not yet received this letter:—

Cawnpore. Aug. 24th 1857.
My dear Colonel,
I have your letter of the 16th inst. I can only say hold on and do not negotiate but rather perish sword in hand. Sir Colin Campbell, who came out at a day's notice to command upon the news arriving of General Anson's death, promised me fresh troops and you will be my first care. The reinforcements may reach me from twenty to twenty-five days and I will prepare everything for a march on Lucknow.
Yours very sincerely, H. Havelock

(Both letters were, for security reasons, written partially in Greek characters.)

6. Brigadier John Inglis wrote:—

Many (of the women), among whom may be mentioned the honoured names of Birch, of Polehampton, of Barber, and of Gall, have, after the example of Miss Nightingale, constituted themselves the tender and solicitous nurses of the wounded and dying soldiers in the hospital.

7. 1846. In consequence of the particularly gallant conduct of Sergeant Bernard M'Cabe, Major-General Sir Henry Smith, in a letter dated 17th February was pleased to recommend him for a commission in the following terms:—

This intrepid non-commissioned officer, in the midst of a hand-to-hand conflict with the enemy, planted the colour of Her Majesty's 31st Regiment upon one of the towers of the enemy's entrenchments—one of the most bold and daring acts of a gallant soldier I ever witnessed, and which, I now deliberately consider, tended much to shorten the struggle alluded to. This sergeant is a young man of excellent character, and, if I may be permitted to remind His Excellency the Commander-in-Chief of the promise made me almost in the heat of battle, it is—'This sergeant shall be recommended for a commission'. I can only add (which is unnecessary to the soldier's friend, Sir Hugh Gough) that, if he receives a commission, it will be as gratifying to me as was the gallant conduct I witnessed at the moment the colour-head was shot off, and the flag perforated with balls, as he triumphantly waved it in the air in the very midst of the enemy.

This highly honourable testimony of the bravery of Sergeant M'Cabe at the Battle of Sobraon, was supported by the strong recommendation of General Lord Gough to his Grace the C.-in-C. Sergeant M'Cabe became an Ensign on 8th May 1846 and transferred to the 32nd some time before April 1849.

8. From Lieut. Edmondstone's letter:—

Havelock's coming in was certainly very dashing but very ill managed. They left their heavy guns in Weston's garden and Lowe had to go out and help to bring them in. Our men formed the rear guard but Napier has given all the credit to Colonel Phurnell. Outram has not given us our due in his account of the proceedings subsequent to the 25 September. Every sortie that was made he ordered to be led by a party of our men and never mentions it.

9. Lieut. Edmondstone's letter tells us:—

On the 29th Sept. sorties were made in all directions in each case led by parties of the 32nd. I with twelve men, all the effective ones remaining in my company, was ordered to lead a sortie towards the Iron Bridge; hundred men of the ——th and thirty of the ——th all under command of Captain S——, ——th. Graydon of the Oude I. Force was sent as a guide. S—— as commanding, in my opinion, ought to have been in front alongside me but thought the rear was the best place and there he stuck and there Graydon and I had to go for him whenever he was wanted. Graydon a very fine fellow stuck alongside throughout the morning. We started before daybreak and got within 100 yards of the bridge without being noticed; one of the men said I can see the guns now about 100 yards off. I said, 'Men there are your guns take them.' They, my men, went down with a cheer, Graydon and I leading them. The enemy let us come within twenty yards when they fired grape into us from both guns and ran for it. A little musketry was opened on us from the houses but did no harm.

We spiked the guns and then turned down the lane leading to Hill's shop and here our misfortunes commenced. A cry commenced amongst the ——th and ——th 'We are being taken in the rear'. I went back and saw it was false so went to the front and went down the lane when a musketry fire was opened on us and which we returned. I proposed charging down the street which the strange men did not like. My poor fellows were awfully disgusted at this saying to one another, 'Did you ever see such a cowardly set?' I said then to Graydon I will go on with our own men. I called 32nd; they gathered round me at once and sprang forward directly I gave the word, the others bringing up the rear. We took three more guns which fired grape into us, also two mortars. Graydon, Private Webster and myself were the first at every gun; at the last gun we had one man hit in four or five places, he was the first that got it.

We then took a 24 lb gun and made preparations to burst it occupying the houses round it. Orders had been given to occupy the houses at the entrance of the lane in order to secure our retreat which Graydon and I thought had been done, the subaltern who got the order confessed to having received it but only said, 'I did not do it.' The gun was burst, the small guns and mortars spiked and we commenced our retreat when a heavy fire was opened upon us from the houses that were ordered to be occupied. We doubled up the street intending to charge the houses and scrag the sepoys; about half way up I got a bullet in the head which floored me and I fell half senseless amongst the ———th men who ran over me never offering to lift me up. I said 'lift me up men' and so I again said 'lift me up for I think I can walk.' No attention was paid, I however contrived to get my hands on to a doorstep and stagger to my feet and walk forward a little where I got hold of a man of my own who took charge of me. We got on till we caught up the leading lot standing under a wall keeping up a fire into the houses. I then saw Graydon. He was bleeding fearfully, and I thought badly hurt, but found it was only a scratch on his ear.

He got a few men together and charged across the road and took possession of the lower parts of the houses, the two men who had me between them carrying me over close after him. There we stood for some time; I was begging the ———th men to take possession of the upper story, but no, they had no appetite for that sort of work. I had two men wounded and two men were employed looking after each wounded man so I could not send the remaining force by themselves up to the top. Graydon begged the other men to follow him up, but no; their officer then ordered them to go up, but did not offer to lead them so they would not stir. I then left them and made the best of my way home, my wound quite unfitting me for any more work. I met Brigadier Inglis one of the first people and told him plainly that the other regiments had not backed me up. Graydon wrote an account of the sortie, but poor fellow he was not so good with his pen as with his sword and made a poor job of it never mentioning a single man, although I know he wrote a letter to Inglis recommending Private Webster of my company for distinguished bravery. Poor Graydon he is dead now and a finer soldier never drew breath but by his not having mentioned my name I do not appear in Inglis' 2nd despatch which is a pity as otherwise I would have had a good chance of my brevet, even now I believe I have a chance. My wound kept me a month in hospital but here I am now all right and junior captain of the 32nd Regiment or as Sir Colin calls us 'the gallant remnant'. I hear we are to be sent home. General Penny has offered me his A.D.C.ship but I cannot possibly leave the regiment now owing to the paucity of officers with the regiment and I cannot expect he will keep it open for me. Francis was killed. Macfarlane was wounded and has gone home sick.

Love to all & believe me,

Your affect, son

John Edmondstone

I have two shawls for you late the property of the King of Oudh.

(Lieutenant John Edmondstone was mentioned in the Governor-General's despatch.)

Lady Inglis, wife of Colonel Inglis, tells us that:—

. . . this last affair of spiking the guns was far from being successful; only seven guns were spiked and our loss was most severe. Poor M'Cabe was carried past our door shot through the lungs. Mr Edmondstone, 32nd, slightly wounded. The latter behaved most bravely, having with three of the 32nd rushed forward to spike a gun when a good many of the others fell back; he and two of the men were hit, the remaining one spiking the gun—an act worthy of the V.C. Cuney and Smith of the 32nd were both killed; two braver men never lived; the former had no right to be out, as he was on the sick list, but he could not resist accompanying the party, as his comrade Smith and he had been together all through the siege.

Captain Birch, in his narrative of the siege of Lucknow, wrote:—

As an example of brilliant courage, which to my mind made him one of the heroes of the siege, I must instance Private Cuney, H.M. 32nd. His exploits were marvellous: he was backed by a sepoy named Kundial, who simply adored him. Single-handed and without any orders, Cuney would go outside our position, and he knew more of the enemy's movements than anyone else. It was impossible to be really angry with him. Over and over again he was put into the guard room for disobedience of orders, and as often let out when there was fighting to be done. On one occasion he surprised one of the enemy's batteries, into which he crawled, followed by his faithful sepoy, bayoneting four men and spiking the guns. He was often wounded, and several times left his bed to volunteer for a sortie.

LEONAUR

ALSO FROM LEONAUR

AVAILABLE IN SOFTCOVER OR HARDCOVER WITH DUST JACKET

WELLINGTON AND THE PYRENEES CAMPAIGN VOLUME I: FROM VITORIA TO THE BIDASSOA *by F. C. Beatson*—The final phase of the campaign in the Iberian Peninsula.

WELLINGTON AND THE INVASION OF FRANCE VOLUME II: THE BIDASSOA TO THE BATTLE OF THE NIVELLE *by F. C. Beatson*—The second of Beatson's series on the fall of Revolutionary France published by Leonaur, the reader is once again taken into the centre of Wellington's strategic and tactical genius.

WELLINGTON AND THE FALL OF FRANCE VOLUME III: THE GAVES AND THE BATTLE OF ORTHEZ *by F. C. Beatson*—This final chapter of F. C. Beatson's brilliant trilogy shows the 'captain of the age' at his most inspired and makes all three books essential additions to any Peninsular War library.

NAVAL BATTLES OF THE NAPOLEONIC WARS *by W. H. Fitchett*—Cape St. Vincent, the Nile, Cadiz, Copenhagen, Trafalgar & Others

SERGEANT GUILLEMARD: THE MAN WHO SHOT NELSON? *by Robert Guillemard*—A Soldier of the Infantry of the French Army of Napoleon on Campaign Throughout Europe

WITH THE GUARDS ACROSS THE PYRENEES *by Robert Batty*—The Experiences of a British Officer of Wellington's Army During the Battles for the Fall of Napoleonic France, 1813.

A STAFF OFFICER IN THE PENINSULA *by E. W. Buckham*—An Officer of the British Staff Corps Cavalry During the Peninsula Campaign of the Napoleonic Wars

THE LEIPZIG CAMPAIGN: 1813—NAPOLEON AND THE "BATTLE OF THE NATIONS" *by F. N. Maude*—Colonel Maude's analysis of Napoleon's campaign of 1813.

BUGEAUD: A PACK WITH A BATON by *Thomas Robert Bugeaud*—The Early Campaigns of a Soldier of Napoleon's Army Who Would Become a Marshal of France.

TWO LEONAUR ORIGINALS

SERGEANT NICOL by *Daniel Nicol*—The Experiences of a Gordon Highlander During the Napoleonic Wars in Egypt, the Peninsula and France.

WATERLOO RECOLLECTIONS by *Frederick Llewellyn*—Rare First Hand Accounts, Letters, Reports and Retellings from the Campaign of 1815.

www.ingramcontent.com/pod-product-compliance
Lightning Source LLC
Chambersburg PA
CBHW021059090426
42738CB00006B/409